PAGAN AND
EARTH-CENTERED VOICES IN
UNITARIAN UNIVERSALISM

Jerrie Kishpaugh Hildebrand and Shirley Ann Ranck
Editors

SKINNER HOUSE BOOKS
BOSTON

www.skinnerhouse.org

Printed in the United States

Cover and text design by Suzanne Morgan

print ISBN: 978-1-55896-795-3
eBook ISBN: 978-1-55896-796-0

6 5 4 3 2 / 20 19 18

Library of Congress Cataloging-in-Publication Data
Names: Kishpaugh Hildebrand, Jerrie, 1955- editor.
Title: Pagan and earth-centered voices in Unitarian universalism / edited by
  Jerrie Kishpaugh Hildebrand and Shirley Ann Ranck.
Description: Boston : Skinner House Books, 2017. | Description based on print
  version record and CIP data provided by publisher; resource not viewed.
Identifiers: LCCN 2017000303 (print) | LCCN 2017011769 (ebook) | ISBN
  9781558967960 | ISBN 9781558967953 (pbk. : alk. paper)
Subjects: LCSH: Nature—Religious aspects. | Religions. | Paganism. |
  Neopaganism. | Unitarian Universalist Association.
Classification: LCC BL435 (ebook) | LCC BL435 .P34 2017 (print) | DDC
  230/.9132—dc23
LC record available at https://lccn.loc.gov/2017000303

We gratefully acknowledge permission to reprint the following:
Excerpt from pp. 102–3 from *The Spiral Dance* by Starhawk, copyright © 1979 by Miriam Simos, reprinted by permission of HarperCollins Publishers; excerpt of 4 lines from "Multicolored Momma" from *Jambalaya: The Natural Woman's Book of Personal Charms and Practical Rituals* by Luisah Teish, copyright © 1985 by Luisah Teish, reprinted by permission of HarperCollins Publishers; "Vibrant, Juicy, Contemporary: Or, Why I Am a UU Pagan" by Margot Adler appeared in *UU World* magazine Nov. 13, 1996, reprinted by permission of her estate.

CONTENTS

Acknowledgments

On February 18, 2014, after we agreed to take on this book project with Skinner House, we met with Starhawk from the Reclaiming Collective in the Bay Area of California, Selena Fox from Circle Sanctuary in Wisconsin, and Margot Adler of New York. All three of these women have built large organizations in the Pagan movement and made huge differences in the landscape of UU Paganism. It was like being at the table with powerful goddesses. It was honoring, affirming, empowering, and prophetic.

As each woman shared their thoughts, we took notes and considered how to collaborate and manage the project. Margot Adler said that it was time for the next set of UU Pagan voices to rise up and share. She was thrilled other UU Pagans would be speaking their thoughts, experiences, and wisdom.

We invited Margot to write for the book given all of the work she has done in the denomination. She suggested we use the article she wrote in 1996 for *UU World*. At this point she knew that she might not be with us when the book was published due to her illness.

Sadly, Margot Adler passed away on July 28, 2014, almost six months after that meeting. Her contributions to Unitarian Universalism will be remembered and serve as inspiration to those who step up now and in the future.

Both of us, as editors, thank all those who wrote essays for this book—your hearts are reflected in the stories you have shared. We also thank our families, who graciously helped us edit and, at times, even typed, for us. We thank Skinner House Books for honoring Paganism and Earth-centered traditions by publishing this book.

For us, all these acts of generosity and voices honor the Earth as sacred, the goddesses and gods, and the Ancient Ones. The circle of wisdom continues. Blessed Be.

Introduction

Hear the words of the Star Goddess, the dust of whose feet are the hosts of heaven, whose body encircles the universe: "I who am the beauty of the green Earth and the white moon among the stars and the mysteries of the waters, I call upon your soul to arise and come unto me. For I am the soul of the nature that gives life to the universe. From Me all things proceed and unto Me they must return. Let My worship be in the heart that rejoices, for behold—all acts of love and pleasure are My rituals. Let there be beauty and strength, power and compassion, honor and humility, mirth and reverence within you. And you who seek to know Me, know that your seeking and yearning will avail you not, unless you know the Mystery: for if that which you seek, you find not within yourself, you will never find it without. For behold, I have been with you from the beginning, and I am that which is attained at the end of desire."

—*Starhawk*

We are honored to offer in this book a taste of the history, beliefs, values, spirituality, and personal journeys of Unitarian Universalists who identify as Pagan or Earth-centered in their spirituality. Beliefs and practices among us vary widely, and the essayists who have graciously agreed to participate in this project share the aspects of these traditions that have been especially meaningful to them, particularly within the context of Unitarian Universalism.

We invite you on a journey with each of our essayists. It takes courage to be known for who you are. These beautiful, loving, and gentle people claim both their Unitarian Universalist and Pagan or Earth-centered heritages, and by doing so challenge both in transformative ways. For that, we thank them and are blessed.

There is no singular tradition associated with Earth-centered spirituality, and it is impossible to say much that is categorically true for all who identify their religious path as such, even under the umbrella of Unitarian Universalism. Even the word *Pagan* is complicated. For some, it refers to the religious traditions of Old Europe and Greece and Rome. For others, it means any tradition outside the Abrahamic three—Judaism, Christianity, and Islam. For still others, it refers to indigenous religions around the world where women and the Earth are still honored.

Many Unitarian Universalists have reclaimed the word *Pagan* to some extent. We have learned that the original word *Paganus* simply meant "country person." As Christianity spread, it was strongest in the cities, and the country people often kept to their own old traditions. So *Pagan* or "country person" gradually became a derogatory term for non-Christians. When we came to discuss the title of this book, we decided to be inclusive and to use both *Pagan* and *Earth-centered* to describe the voices included.

But what unites everyone with different belief systems and practices who identity with either of these terms within Unitarian Universalism? Broadly stated, we place a special emphasis in our spiritual lives on the feminine aspect of divinity, the cycles of nature, the honoring of our ancestors, and the inherent divine and creative potential in all people.

There is meaningful overlap between this last idea— what we might call the internalization of religion—and the values, culture, and beliefs of Unitarian Universalism. Contemporary Pagans speak of the God or Goddess within each of us. We practice a religion that places divinity within each person. Myths are accepted as ways of telling the story of our inner journeys. Each person is encouraged to explore their own experience and to find there the basis for values and commitments. Since the divine is experienced as internal, it is described in female as well as male terms.

Folks who call themselves Pagan or Earth-centered tend to believe that, just as the divine is within human beings in the shape of our creativity, so too is it immanent in all of nature. And like Unitarian Universalists, we see ourselves as interdependent or connected with every part of the natural world. We place particular spiritual value on celebrating the cycles of nature, the seasons, the waxing and waning of the moon, the life stages of human beings. For many Unitarian Universalists, Christmas has become a celebration of the winter solstice and Easter a celebration of spring. In moving away from the idea of a divine savior, we have returned to the more ancient awareness of religion as the way we affirm our position within the cycles of the natural world.

Another characteristic of Pagan and Earth-based religions is our non-authoritarian attitude. "Do as you will as long as you harm no one" is the rule of Pagan religion. Leadership is shared and there is no hierarchy. Freedom and responsibility for one's own life and beliefs are central, just as they are for Unitarian Universalists, allowing the creativity within each person to be tapped and fostering the creation of new poetry, new meditations, new stories. This means, of course, that the leadership and creativity of women is valued equally with that of men.

Our History

When Unitarians and Universalists merged in 1961, they agreed to co-create a living tradition that would draw from many sources for wisdom and inspiration. The original list of five Sources included not only Jewish and Christian teachings in which both Unitarianism and Universalism had roots but other world religions and humanist teachings as well. The door seemed open for us to find inspiration in many places and perhaps add to the list of Sources.

In the years that followed, two major movements emerged within Unitarian Universalism—feminism and ecology. Unitarian Universalist women began to reclaim and celebrate both ancient and modern indigenous or "Pagan" myths about the divine imagined as female. These myths were not about supernatural beings but were wonderful stories of women's power and creativity. And both women and men, facing a growing ecological crisis, began to recognize and celebrate the honoring of the Earth in these same traditions.

Many Unitarian Universalists then suggested that we add Pagan traditions to our official list of Sources. But the word *Pagan* was tainted. It had for too long been used as a derogatory term, and thousands of people labeled as Pagan had been murdered over the centuries. The debate at General Assembly over this possible sixth Source was heated until Rev. Paul L'Herrou suggested that we refer to these traditions as *Earth-centered* rather than *Pagan*. The 1995 resolution, listing a sixth Source as "spiritual teachings of Earth-centered traditions which celebrate the sacred circle of life and instruct us to live in harmony with the rhythms of nature," then passed with great support.

It is also important to understand that our seventh Principle, affirming respect for "the interdependent web of all existence of which we are a part," was included in the 1985 adoption of the Principles and Purposes. Unitarian Universalists embraced the sciences of the twentieth century, sciences that indicated that humans were not separate from the rest of nature but rather a part of the web. We had begun to realize that if we damage any part of that web, we damage ourselves. The seventh Principle and the sixth Source are at the heart of Unitarian Universalist involvement with Pagan or Earth-centered traditions.

The advent of UU Pagans, one could say, started with the advent of feminist theology in the 1980s. The UU Continental Feminist Convocation, the Women and Religion Committee, and other groups of women began to study the notion of a feminine side of the sacred. They studied goddesses, wrote books on feminist theology, and invited speakers on the subject to General Assembly. They wrote religious-education materials on the subject of the Goddess. With this came an acknowledgment of the ties of goddesses to Pagan and Earth-centered faith and spiritual traditions.

This idea of the divine feminine brought new people to congregations, where they practiced these old but new ways to worship and honor Spirit. In 1985, a small group gathered to look into forming an independent affiliate for Pagans within the denomination. Later that year, this group would go to a meeting of the Covenant of the Goddess and introduce UU Paganism to the larger Pagan movement. They chose the name Covenant of Unitarian Universalist Pagans (CUUPS), which played off of the flaming chalice, the symbol of Unitarian Universalism. They used the image of two flaming chalices side by side to represent the two "U"s of Unitarian Universalism. In 1988, CUUPS received independent affiliate status at General Assembly.

In 1986, Unitarian Universalist minister Christa Heiden Landon founded Panthea Pagan Temple. When that congregation attempted to affiliate with the UUA, it encountered some public opposition. Unitarian Universalists on both sides of the debate came together to find common ground. Ultimately, delegates voted to accept the congregation's request and Panthea Temple became the first UU congregation rooted in Pagan traditions to affiliate with the denomination.

That same year, Beacon Press, which is owned by the UUA, published a revised edition of *Drawing Down the Moon: Witches, Druids, Goddess-Worshippers, and Other Pagans in America Today* by NPR reporter Margot Adler. A priestess in the Gardnerian Wiccan Tradition and member of the Unitarian Church of All Souls in New York City, Adler supported UU Paganism and spoke at many UU gatherings and churches, and wrote occasionally for *UU World*. In 1993, the new hymnal, *Singing the Living Tradition*, included readings by Starhawk, one of Adler's contemporaries, as well as Earth-centered chants and hymns.

UU Pagans in the early 1990s began to work with the larger Pagan movement regarding social justice and religious freedom issues. Some UU Pagans stood at the forefront of these issues with other national Pagan organizations. These cases ranged from custody battles to supporting young people in schools who fought for the right to honor their holy days. Many UU Pagans took on the federal government, advocating for the right of Pagan veterans to have their sacred symbols on government-issued headstones.

UU Pagans continue to make an impact with our efforts today. We are creating educational materials about nature-centered thea/ology resources for both the Pagan and Unitarian Universalist communities. We are teaching in seminaries, becoming ministers or ordained priests and priestesses, and bringing our skills in organizational development to a religious movement that has grown by leaps and bounds.

The future of UU Paganism is bright. We are making a real difference and are doing our part to transform the world. Our activities remind us of how one person's voice—and our collective voice—can call many to the table of understanding.

For most of the contributors to this book, Unitarian Universalism and their Pagan or Earth-based spirituality are interwoven. We hope you will get an enhanced sense of the richness of both traditions and enrich your personal spiritual journey as well. We have enjoyed putting together this book about the traditions we love, and we hope that love comes through.

A Unitarian Universalist Journey into Paganism

Shirley Ann Ranck

*The image of the Goddess inspires women to see ourselves
as divine, our bodies as sacred, the changing phases of
our lives as holy.*

—Starhawk

At Starr King School for the Ministry in the late 1970s,
my dear friend Rev. Chris Bailey came running in from the
library one day exclaiming, "Look, look what I found!"
She held up a recording. Archaeologists had found ancient
clay tablets with unusual markings as well as words. They
figured out that it was musical notation, and that the
words were a hymn to the Moon Goddess. The scholars
constructed a lyre similar to the kind that was used at the
time of the tablets and played and sang the hymn for the
recording. Listening to that music, preserved for us across
more than three millennia, was a sacred moment.

I personally came to the old Pagan religions as a woman searching for my female religious history. My interest in these traditions began when our Unitarian Universalist General Assembly unanimously passed a Women and Religion Resolution in 1977. It demanded that we, as a religious people professing the inherent worth and dignity of every person, examine our theologies, our language, and our organizational structures in order to root out sexism in every area of our religious life.

I was in Berkeley, California, at Starr King School for the Ministry at the time, and I became involved in the work of the district Women and Religion Task Force as we tried to implement the resolution. It was an exciting time as we planned women's retreats and encouraged each other to challenge the sexist language in worship and to claim our own voices and power. But something was missing. If we no longer referred to the divine as "Lord" or "King" or with only masculine pronouns, did that mean that the divine was in fact female?

Starr King provided me and others an opportunity to research in some depth the roots of women's religious history in pre-historic and early historic times when the divine was almost universally imaged as female. It is difficult to convey in words the excitement that some of us women theological students felt as we began to unearth our own religious heritage. Rev. Emily Champagne, who had graduated from Starr King in the sixties, returned to do some research. She discovered Enheduanna, a real high

priestess, poet, and thealogian who lived in the ancient
Sumerian city of Ur about 2360 BCE and wrote a series of
hymns to the goddess Inanna. Why, we wondered, had we
heard nothing about her in our regular classes?

It is difficult to describe the intense shock of recogni-
tion and anger that I felt as a woman at the moment when
I realized that in contrast to Christians, who worship a
divine father and son, the pilgrims who made their way to
Eleusis for two thousand or more years worshipped a divine
mother and *daughter*. The medium is indeed the message.
All the teachings of love and justice in the world could not
erase or make up for the stark and overwhelming absence
of the divine female in my Protestant Christian upbringing.

Try to grasp the immensity of the fact that the chief
divine actors in this drama were a mother and her daughter.
The myth of Persephone's journey has its antecedents in
the spiritual quest of the Sumerian goddess Inanna, who
also descended to the underworld. Persephone decides she
must leave her mother and embark on her own spiritual
journey. Only in later patriarchal versions of the myth is
she carried off by force. Ultimately Persephone returns to
her mother, Demeter, transformed into an adult by her
journey, and they rejoice in a new kind of relationship.

As we continued our research we learned that our sacred
history as women is a story grounded in the findings of
modern archaeology and anthropology. At the same time
it is a story that transcends those findings as it serves a
mythic function in our lives. Great myths reflect and teach

us many truths about ourselves, our history, and our society. Divine power, the power of life and death, was for many thousands of years thought to be female.

Distinguished archaeologists such as Raphael Patai, Rachel Levy, and Marija Gimbutas told us that for many thousands of years human beings worshipped this divine mother. As renowned mythologist Joseph Campbell opined in his book *The Masks of God*, "There can be no doubt that in the very earliest ages of human history, the magical force and wonder of the female was no less a marvel than the universe itself and this gave to women a prodigious power."

Pagans, they were called, those Greeks and Romans, as well as Canaanites, Egyptians, and Old Europeans who worshipped goddesses. As a woman I needed to claim that heritage. I needed to know that great civilizations were created by people who worshipped the divine as female. If the myths of a culture reflect its social arrangements, women must have had power and respect.

As I absorbed these learnings I felt deeply empowered as a woman. I was consumed by a passion to know my female religious roots—mythic goddesses of the Ancient Near East, strong women of ancient Judaism and in the early Christian church, the elevation of Mary to larger-than-life status, powerful goddesses of Asia, Africa, and the indigenous religions of the Americas. I also wanted to know how and why the power of the sacred female had been edited out of my own Western traditions.

While I was still at Starr King I attended a conference at the University of California at Santa Cruz. There I first experienced a Pagan ritual led by Z. Budapest. I also heard Carol Christ's talk "Why Women Need the Goddess," and suddenly all my training in psychology was both drawn upon and challenged by my spiritual journey as a woman. To imagine the divine as female meant that my body was sacred. To imagine the divine as female meant that the bond between mothers and daughters was holy, not a source of resentment and hostility. To imagine the divine as female meant that real women like me had inherent power. To imagine the divine as female meant that women could act on our own behalf. I was exhilarated by these discoveries. They seemed to confirm some deep inner knowledge I had glimpsed but never quite trusted: my own competence and power, my own strength of will, my own body as a source of life and nurture. I wanted other women to be empowered by these insights.

When I returned to my typing job in one of the Graduate Theological Union (GTU) offices, the philosophy professor Jacob Needleman stopped by one day to tell us about a large grant he had received to study new religious movements in America. He said he had distributed some of the money to students who were interviewing and writing about various gurus. I asked him if anyone was studying the Goddess religion that was becoming popular among many women. He said no, and asked me to tell him about it. I told him about the conference. He said that if I would write a paper and teach a course at the GTU about the Goddess religion, he could offer me a grant of $1,000. I accepted the offer with great excitement, and about a dozen women from various theological schools registered for the course.

In 1980 I was given another opportunity. Rev. Leslie Westbrook was on the UUA staff in Boston and was charged with implementing the 1977 Women and Religion resolution. She called and asked me if I would like to write a study guide in feminist theology. I met with her in Boston and also attended the UU Women's Convocation in East Lansing, Michigan. Over the next few months, the more Leslie and I talked, the larger our project seemed to get, and the more controversial it became. We had it designed within a year, but because of difficulties in obtaining permission to use our many resources, and because of various strong criticisms, five years went by before it was published. During that time Leslie left the UUA to start her family and Elizabeth Anastos took over the job of trying to get our feminist theology project published. After much discussion and some minor changes, Elizabeth was successful and *Cakes for the Queen of Heaven* was finally published by the UUA in 1986. It came in a beautifully decorated box that contained a manual of ten sessions, a booklet of additional resource articles, three Beacon Press books, and a filmstrip. When I received it I sat for a long time, treasuring it with tears in my eyes.

As I studied the ancient goddesses and the old religions, I learned that they honored the Earth as well as women. When women's groups made that discovery they often began to meet outdoors on beaches, in the woods, or high on hilltops to celebrate the phases of the moon, the solstices, and the spring and fall equinoxes, reclaiming our connection to the natural world. They uncovered a pressing and passionate need for such connectedness. Both women and men became advocates for the environment.

As a mostly urban person, I was shocked to find myself in a Midwestern meadow doing a spiral dance in the moonlight, or seated in a circle around a bonfire on a hillside overlooking San Francisco Bay. In the process, I changed. I returned to the New Jersey beaches of my youth, felt the pull of the ocean currents, the thrill of diving beneath a monster wave, the breathtaking beauty of a silvery path across the water to the moon. I also wept at how often *No Swimming* signs were placed on the beaches because pollution had reached dangerous levels. I rediscovered my personal connection with nature. The process of creating and teaching *Cakes for the Queen of Heaven* made me aware that a whole new thea/ology and worldview might be emerging in our postmodern world.

Perhaps the most satisfying result of the *Cakes* course for me has been the hundreds of individual women who have written or spoken to me about their personal experience with the course. Women of many ages, many levels of education, many kinds of lives, yet each in her own way has said the same thing: It changed my life. The tribute so many women have paid to *Cakes* has affirmed me powerfully as a person and as a minister.

—◦—

SHIRLEY ANN RANCK *is a retired Unitarian Universalist minister who has touched the lives of many women with her feminist thealogy curriculum and book* Cakes for the Queen of Heaven. *She is a Crone, and her book* The Grandmother Galaxy *tells the story of her journey into feminist spirituality.*

VIBRANT, JUICY, CONTEMPORARY: OR, WHY I AM A UU PAGAN

MARGOT ADLER

When I was five, I asked my father what religion we were. An atheist from a nominally Jewish background, he told me, "We believe in the brotherhood of man." Now, this did not cut it for a five-year-old, particularly when my best friend got to put on her white dress and have holy communion. Feeling she was getting a much better deal, I demanded that my father start to read me the Bible. And I wanted to be a Catholic.

Meanwhile, my mother was also saying, "You're Jewish," and my father was saying, "No, we're not." So I come from a background of religious confusion and even conflict. My father, although Jewish, had actually been brought up in a Lutheran household. He had never been circumcised, and he celebrated Christmas—a tradition my family continued.

Then two things happened that really affected me spiritually. First, when I was ten years old, our entire class went out very early on May 1 to the country house of our teacher's sister. We had learned all these medieval May Day carols, and as the sun rose, we started singing them and picking flowers. We took armfuls of flowers back to New York and threw them around the school, singing the medieval May Day carols. Then we danced around the maypole. And I became a ritual junkie for life.

Then we studied ancient Greece for the entire seventh grade. This was in 1957, and there weren't a lot of powerful images of women in the society to help young girls think about who and what they wanted to be. But I was reading about Artemis and Athena, these incredible Greek goddesses. I decided way down deep I didn't want to worship them, I wanted to be them. They were the most powerful images of confidence and inner strength I had seen in the society I was growing up in.

But, by the time I was fourteen, I realized you do not go around worshiping the Greek gods or pretending you are them without ending up in a mental hospital. So I hid this stuff in psychic storage, you might say, and went on with my life.

Then, in 1970, right around the time of the first Earth Day, I started reading the nature writers—Thoreau, Loren Eiseley, Rene Dubos, and Rachel Carson. Although I found myself excited and energized by the ecology movement, my response to these writings was not entirely political. As I read these writers, I was having what I can only describe now as religious feelings. I saw that this literature was about our whole relationship to the universe; it showed that everything was interconnected. It helped me understand my place in the universe in a way I had never understood it before.

Soon after that, I came across two essays that profoundly affected me: "The Religious Roots of Our Environmental Crisis" by Arnold Toynbee, and "The Historic Roots of Our Ecologic Crisis" by Lynn White. These two essays said to me—although I'm simplifying greatly here—that there was a problem with the command in Genesis to "be fruitful and multiply and have dominion over the Earth." This notion put human beings above nature, thereby giving us license to destroy the Earth. The essays also talked about the older Pagan, animistic traditions and their different notions of the divine—that it was present in everything and that everything was alive and vital. I began to think that this older perspective gave one a more sacred sense of the planet and a reluctance to destroy the Earth. I thought, "That's what I have always believed." And I started looking for an ecological religion.

I did really silly things. I went to England, and I looked under "Druids" in the telephone directory. Actually, there was a Druid Order, a masonic-type group that would go to Stonehenge and parade around on the solstice in white robes. But they were not exactly what I was looking for.

But slowly I became aware of an entire movement— which, for better or worse, I will call the Earth-centered traditions—including anything from indigenous traditions to contemporary Pagan forms, to people who are reviving

the Goddess spirituality movement, to Wicca, to people
who are reviving Nordic religions, to people who are
looking at what their ancestors were involved in 3,000 or
4,000 or 5,000 years ago and trying to create that again in
a contemporary form.

Through a fluke I got a book contract, as a result of
which I ended up going around the country and finding
all sorts of Pagan groups. Of course, Paganism today is a
minority religious tradition, and it will probably never be a
majority tradition in this country. It doesn't even see itself
as being the religion for everyone. Instead, it sees itself as
one among many jewels. But it has certain insights that are
useful for anyone about living in this world.

Now, it's easy to grow up in the United States and think
of religion as what I call the Big Five: Christianity, Judaism,
Islam, Hinduism, Buddhism. Most religions we're familiar with have many similarities. They have, for example,
written scripture. They have, for example, prophets—wise
men, usually—who've come down to tell humans about
how to live their lives. They have rules, and many of
them—definitely Christianity and Islam—see themselves
as universal religions—that is, as appropriate for all people
and places. In fact, certain traditions within Christianity
and Islam believe it's a duty to proselytize because their
religion is the universal truth, appropriate for everyone.
I think we've grown up thinking these characteristics—
things like scripture, creed, rules, and prophets—are what
makes up a religion.

But the traditions I'm talking about don't have any of these characteristics. They don't have written scripture. They don't have a very well-formed creed. Rather, these religions, which were the religions of our ancestors 40,000 years ago, are based on practice, as opposed to belief. They are based on experience. What do we do to make the crops grow? How do we commemorate a young son's coming of age? How do we bring healing to our community? What is the custom here? What is appropriate for this occasion? How do we tie ourselves into celestial happenings or the seasons? These questions are all based on community and seasonal cycles—the doing, the planting, the harvesting—and not based on creed or written scripture. Interestingly, Judaism, which is of course a tribal religion at its base, has a lot of those same things. You don't have to believe in God to be a Jew. You're part of a tribe. I was brought up as a completely atheistic Jew, and yet I was still a Jew.

Indigenous religion, like Judaism, is not universal; it's based on place. Native American nations and cultures have their sacred mountains, their sacred spots, just as Jews have the land of Israel. Indigenous traditions don't get involved in proselytizing because they don't assume that other people should be part of their religious tradition. This is a huge notion, because if you don't proselytize, then how can you have a religious war?

Another thing I found was that, because these traditions were not universal, were based on oral tradition and not the written word, they were much more metaphorical and theologically more flexible. There would never be a creationism-vs.-science dispute in Paganism. The Pagan point of view would be, "Well, yes, there is that dream reality of my creation myth, and then there's modern science, and well, yeah, they're multiple realities—both are real. But they're different parts of my reality. I can dance around a bonfire at night, and then the next day, I can go to work as a computer programmer." It's a more metaphoric than literal notion of reality, very different from religions that are tied to scripture.

But as I get older, I no longer believe in almost any "either-or." I now believe almost everything is "both-and." Many dichotomies are nonsense when you think deeply about them: male and female, dark and light, material and spiritual. Any mystic knows that. Take Teresa of Avila. She knew that when you wash the dishes, that is part of a spiritual experience. Even the whole notion—here's something I shouldn't say as a good liberal—the whole notion of church-state separation is ridiculous. At least cognitively. Of course, it's important because I wouldn't want to be a non-Christian in a Christian nation, so maybe we have to do it politically. But the idea that religious reality and political reality are separate? Ridiculous!

The same goes for the idea that humor and religion don't mix. If you visit the Kung bushmen, you might see a ceremony in which they're trance-dancing for two days, and then in the middle of the ceremony someone might make a joke with some sexual connotations about the man dancing, and he makes a little comment and then goes right back into his trance—and there's a sense that there's no difference. I once went into a Zen garden in Japan, and suddenly a loud troop of Japanese schoolchildren came romping through, and I thought, "They're ruining my mystical experience, these children!" But then I backtracked and said, "I'm wrong! This, too, is part of sacred reality."

Consistent with the lack of separation between the sacred and profane is the Earth-centered traditions' understanding of deity as immanent, in everything. This means that not only is the mind holy but the body is holy, sexuality is holy, everything is a piece, and it's all part of the sacred reality. All this boils down to what I would call an ecological perspective on religion. One-crop economies always fail, and a healthy meadow, a healthy forest always has multiple species living interdependently. It may be heretical and subversive, but I think spiritual reality should be like that—that, again, we're all not supposed to arrive at one answer, that maybe the world could be richer, deeper, more interesting because, in fact, there are many answers and that only if we each seek out our own answers will we be able to chart a path through the dark days that seem to lie ahead.

Another thing attracting me to Earth-centered traditions goes back to what I said about my early attraction to the Greek goddesses. So many women are coming to the Goddess spirituality movement. This is happening both outside and inside organized religion, and it's happening in Judaism and Christianity, as well as Paganism.

For example, the United Church of Christ came out with a prayer book a couple of years ago that included words like "O, God, from the womb of your being. . . ." Within Judaism, women are holding "New Moon circles" and doing serious research into the feminine aspect of the divine, the pre-Canaanite goddesses and their roles. In our own Unitarian Universalist Association, there is, of course, the study guide called *Cakes for the Queen of Heaven* that started going around in 1986. This look at the ancient goddesses and what they mean has transformed Unitarian Universalism from a heady, sometimes overly rationalist group into a group that is more open to exuberant ritual.

Why has this movement taken on such force? Why are there hundreds of books being published on Goddess spirituality? Why are so many women finding themselves attracted to it? What is going on here? I think the main reason women are coming to Paganism is that, in many denominations, they've been left out. They've been robbed of their chance for ministry. There are so many frustrated would-be Catholic priests in the Goddess spirituality movement, it's amazing.

But the history of the women's spirituality movement goes back to the women's consciousness-raising groups of the 1960s and early 1970s. Think about what happened there. In the group I belonged to, we sat in a circle and spoke on a topic that was decided the week before—things like high school, my first menstruation, my mother, sexuality. Ten, twelve women sat around a circle. Each one spoke for, let's say, seven or eight minutes, and no one interrupted—that was very important because twenty-five years ago a woman couldn't sit on a park bench and read a book or sit in a restaurant alone and not be interrupted.

So this was the first time many of these women could actually speak from the inner self without being interrupted. The big idea that came out of the consciousness-raising groups was that the personal was political—that from your personal experience—with high school, your mother, the men in your life—came an understanding of the world and politics.

When that point had been made, women started doing other things. They said, "Well, if the personal is political, maybe the personal is spiritual, too," and so women started spiritual groups, where they talked about their dreams in the same way they'd been talking about politics, and they asked: "Why are women always called witches? Why are they always seen as evil?" They looked into the history of midwife persecution and the devaluation of women's wisdom and healing. They said, "Well, maybe because these people were on the outs with society and were independent-minded, they got called witches, but really they were just doing their own things in their own way. Maybe that's what we are, and maybe if I just say, 'I'm a Witch, I'm a Witch, I'm a Witch' three times, I'm really a Witch and that's all it means." So the first women's Witch covens started.

Meanwhile, there was a revival of Paganism that came from people in the folklore movement and people who were researching their own ancestral traditions. It had thousands of followers, which is very small compared to any other religion in America, but it was growing.

It was all in reaction to what I would call our white bread culture. Most of us do come from traditions that are vibrant and juicy. That's for a good reason: our parents, most of them, were immigrants to this country. Many fled oppression. Others were forcibly brought here against their will, in chains. Or they were the native people who were forced into conversion. So, in a sense, we all had Earth-based traditions ripped from us. Of course, some of those traditions were fairly oppressive. In my mother's tradition, boys got the 50-cent Hebrew instructor who taught you meaning of the words, and girls got the 25-cent Hebrew instructor who taught you to mouth the syllables. But these traditions, for all their shortcomings, did have a juicy relationship to the Earth. They had songs, they had stories, they had lullabies, they had ceremonies, they had dances. Very often, by contrast, the religion we've been brought up in is fairly white bread. You know, you sit there in the pew and some minister or rabbi lectures at you.

So there's a huge religious revival in our country—Christian, Jewish, Pagan, whatever—that's partly due to a hunger for the juice of ecstatic spiritual experience, a hunger for a deeper relationship to the Earth, family, community, etcetera. You may search for those roots in many ways. A Christian might look for an ecstatic, evangelical relationship to Christianity, or you may say, "I am Welsh, and my ancestors were Pagans, and I would like to research that and create new ceremonies for that."

So a lot of the Pagan movement today, including a lot of the Wicca movement, is based on going back to our ancestors' traditions or creating them anew—since many of these traditions have been lost. It's an attempt to create a vibrant, juicy contemporary culture based on old sources, on what our ancestors were doing, or at least part of what they were doing, or at least a tiny slice of what they were doing thousands of years ago, but it's also an attempt to bring these traditions into contemporary reality, in ways that are in keeping with democracy and freedom.

Now that I've told you how wonderful these Earth-centered traditions are, you may be wondering why I became a Unitarian Universalist. If the Pagan and Goddess traditions were giving me so much, why did I need an official religion, let alone a church! Goddess help us!

To be truthful about it, not everything comes from personal experience and revelation. There are times when gut and heart and intuition are not enough. Remember Freud's famous saying "Sometimes a cigar is only a cigar?" As I grow older, I realize I'm still very much a child of my skeptical, rationalist upbringing. I'm still very much a materialist. I believe the things of this world and this existence matter, that matter matters, and that the sacred resides in the here and now. I love the fact that Unitarian Universalists have a good many atheists and humanists among them. After all, it's important to have a reality check, to have people who will bring us down to Earth and say, "Stop all this intuitive garbage and look at the reality: this is a ceiling, this is a table, this is a floor. And by the way, get out of that trance: look at that homeless guy lying in the street."

I guess I chose Unitarian Universalism because I need to live in balance. I can do all those wonderful, Earth-centered spiritual things: sing under the stars, drum for hours, create moving ceremonies for the changes of seasons or the passage of time in the lives of men and women. But I also need to be a worldly, down-to-Earth person in a complicated world—someone who believes oppression is real, that tragedies happen, that chaos happens, that not everything is for a purpose. Unitarian Universalism gives me a place to be at home with some of my closest friends: my doubts. Of course, there are many rationalists within the Earth-centered community, but somehow I feel more centered in this denomination. And I think, in turn, the Pagan community has brought to Unitarian Universalism the joy of ceremony, and a lot of creative and artistic ability that will leave the denomination with a richer liturgy and a bit more juice and mystery.

◄◦►

MARGOT ADLER *(1946–2014) was a journalist and correspondent for National Public Radio and the author of* Drawing Down the Moon: Witches, Druids, Goddess-Worshippers, and Other Pagans in America Today, *among other books. She was a Wiccan Priestess in Gardnerian Wicca in the Protean line, a member of the board of trustees of CUUPS, and a member of The Unitarian Church of All Souls in New York City.*

Paths and Patterns

Misty Sheehan

I have a path in my life, and I always know when I am on that path and when I am not. My path, like most people's, is uphill and filled with stones and scratchy sticks. I climb and reach a resting place where I can look out over what I have accomplished, then climb again until I reach another resting place. Paganism has helped me stay on that path.

I read Starhawk and Z. Budapest back in the 1970s and put together a Pagan circle that met on a friend's farm. I set up an altar where I meditated every day. My friends and I had a wild time at our meetings—very free and open. That meditation helped me get through a divorce and a change from homemaker to professor.

Pagan values can be found wherever we search for wisdom. To me, Paganism is not a faith but a variety of paths we can travel to search for our own individual truths that will strengthen us, enable us to grow, and help us to be good citizens of our world. Paganism helps us stay close to nature and feel the call to protect it—from fracking, pollution, and corporate policies that don't consider nature's intrinsic value. Paganism opens us to the patterns and waves of nature, through which we can learn to sing with it. It provides a sense of the creation of the Earth and stars as a feminine caring similar to a mother's fondness toward the kicks of her child in the womb. Paganism gives us the gift of magic if we are open to it.

Being a Part of Nature

For ancient Pagans, understanding the patterns of nature was crucial to survival. The ancient Irish built stone circles across the southern shore of Ireland—some oriented to the winter solstice, some to the summer solstice, and some to the equinoxes. That pattern of light across the skies symbolized other patterns in nature—the growing and death of trees and other vegetation, and the life cycles of the animals. Knowing all this was crucial to good hunting and good harvests.

My Universalist minister at East Liberty Universalist church was a farmer's wife who preached about the patterns of life in the cycle of the seasons. I too felt close to the life around me and learned its patterns. I raised my children in Jackson, Michigan, where we could ski all winter with our dog breaking a trail ahead or running behind us. We saw hollows where deer had slept, as well as coyote and squirrel tracks. We heard the chickadees, blue jays, and cardinals calling back and forth.

Many years later I was teaching in Chicago, away from the natural life forces that I had come into contact with in Michigan. One of my students said, "It just doesn't seem right. I leave my apartment, get in my car, and drive to college. Then I get out of my car and go to class, then return again. It seems like I am missing something in life." I was missing something too. I rode my bike on the bike trails, but they passed through subdivisions that had TruGreen grass, which was treated with chemicals once a week.

But I returned to Michigan several times a year to camp in the wild Sleeping Bear Sand Dunes. After ten years away, I retired back to my beloved forest. From the front of my house, all I see are a meadow and Douglas Fir trees. All I hear are the birds. My neighbors are Tank the badger, Artemis the deer, her twins Romulus and Remus, a bear, and raccoons. And then the small creatures: the squirrels, chipmunks, voles, and mice that hide in the grass. And then the insects that fertilize my flowers, and who crawl under the leaves and stems, and among the roots of my vegetation.

Beloved Unitarian Universalist songwriter Carolyn McDade is one of my most important spiritual teachers. Her music has turned in the last few years to focus on understanding and praising our connection with nature. She feels the patterns, the waves of sunlight, the sound of the wind, and the song of the trees and birds.

Carolyn wants us to understand that we come from the stars, that our connection with life goes back, back, through all the processes the Earth has gone through—from the beginning of the first life in the sea through the chaotic present day. She speculates that long before the creation of the Earth, there was a sense of love that designed the Earth and that we can call on in our relations with others. She calls that spirit "She" as her love gives birth to us all. She says, "We have only begun to love this Earth," and that we should "listen, listen" to those waves from our own bodies and from others to understand the song of the continents. My friend and I, when we go on our weekly walk, will stop and sing, "Stand here, till all you were has wandered away." In our silence, we hear the chickadees and ravens calling to one another, and we feel the energy emanating from the forest around us. We become part of the forest. Then we go on.

Woman as Goddess

In the religious tradition in which I was raised, the idea of a female deity was foreign. I tried to find God within myself, but he did not exist there. More importantly, a Goddess did. I could feel her hands reaching out to become my hands, her feet to become my strength, and her thoughts to become my thoughts.

The goddess who means the most to me is the Hindu goddess Shakti. I learned about her while reading for my doctorate in Hindu philosophy. Shakti is the originator of the waves that make up our lives—waves of wind, waves of water, and the pulsation of blood that runs through our bodies. In atomic science, our bodies are made up of atoms that are made up of electrons and protons and neutrons that can be perceived as either matter or waves. These waves of energy unite us with all other beings, and we can use intuition and yoga to sense and work with these waves. Working with the *kundalini*, the energy that moves up our spinal column into six different *chakras*, or wheels of energy in the body, can strengthen our body and our intuitive faculties to understand better other beings with whom we coexist, and to ultimately comprehend the energy that Shakti is. I did this in yogic meditation through exercises in *pranayama*, or breathing exercises.

This is Hindu philosophy, but it harmonizes with other ancient beliefs that Pagans often gravitate toward. Consider the ancient Celts, who built stone circles along the southern coast of Ireland, each facing another aspect of the sunlight that shines down on us in a pattern of light waves, mingling with sound waves and water waves, patterns of interconnected life itself.

Magic

As a scholar, I respect the scientific method of experimentation, but there is much in life that can't be explained by science, and we can call that magic. We don't know why magic happens. Sometimes it can be thought of as intuition, that aspect of learning that can't be verified by experimentation but is nonetheless a valid part of knowledge. And sometimes magic, like intuition, just happens.

For instance, I made an agreement with a friend of mine in India that we would meditate once a month at the same time to see if we could pass thoughts and information to each other. We emailed each other immediately after the meditation. We found that sending messages in words didn't work, but sending thoughts and feelings did. The Chinese traditions tai chi and qigong affirm the potential of such transmissions.

People can influence others positively through meditation. At an ashram I once visited in India, one of the nuns was believed to be enlightened. My friend and I arranged a conversation with her. While she was speaking, we both felt as if we had been meditating for hours. The energy in our centers moved around, bubbled up, and created infinite peace. We both agreed she was on a different level than we were to be able to influence us so positively and strongly. Enlightenment in Hinduism is the creation of wisdom within oneself. The enlightened nun was wise to the patterns within each of us that she touched.

Sometimes things are just magic. One summer solstice, I was having lunch with five friends at a picnic table in a backyard. We saw a stag with a full head of antlers cross the front yard of my friend's country home. The stag crashed through the forsythia bushes, a representation of the male force of nature, then disappeared in front of the house. He balanced our feminine intuition with the strength of male energy, also necessary for life. A biologist friend said it was impossible, that bucks don't have all their antlers that early in the season, but six of us saw it. As a vision, this impossibility concretized the importance of the stag to me.

Paganism has created the patterns that have led me on my path of life. My pattern is not another's pattern, however. We each seek our own sense of understanding. Paganism has taught me that, though we all are different, we are made up of those waves. It has taught me that the Earth and all its beings need to be respected. And it has taught me that the feminine in each of us needs to be respected in order to find full meaning in life.

—◦—

MISTY SHEEHAN *is a professor at Northwestern Michigan College, teaching Eastern and Western Religion and Ethics. She first became a Pagan in 1973 and was a high priestess of a coven. She is now a solo practitioner. Her academic career has taken her to India, where she lived for one year, and to China, where she lived for four years.*

CELEBRATING SEASONS

SELENA FOX

Winter solstice approaches. Also known as Yule, it is the time of longest nights and shortest days. Pagans gather in living rooms, Unitarian Universalist meeting halls, ancient stone circles, present-day Pagan temples, and a host of other places to celebrate the winter solstice and the start of the new solar year. Celebrations include a variety of customs, from decorating evergreens and singing songs to lighting candles and spending time in quiet reflection. Although Yule observances vary by location and the participants involved, observing the winter solstice serves several purposes to strengthen bonds with others, deepen connections with nature's rhythms, and continue widespread traditions and celebrations. Many Christmas and New Year's customs are rooted in the winter solstice celebrations of ancient Pagans.

In addition to winter solstice, Pagans celebrate changes in the cycle of the sun and seasons throughout the year.

Most Pagans call their calendar of seasonal holidays the "Wheel of the Year." It includes the solstices and equinoxes, which mark the beginnings of the four seasons. These are the winter solstice (Yule), spring equinox (Ostara), summer solstice (Litha), and fall equinox (Mabon). The Wheel of the Year also includes the midpoints of each season, known as the Cross Quarter Days and the Celtic Fire Festivals: Imbolc (middle of winter), Beltane (middle of spring), Lughnassadh (middle of summer), and Samhain (middle of autumn). All eight seasonal holidays are known as Sabbats.

Celebrating a seasonal festival every six to seven weeks strengthens Pagans' awareness of and spiritual connection to the greater circle of nature. Making time, at regular intervals, for these sacred practices is a wonderful approach and opportunity to shift from a human-centric consciousness to an eco-centric consciousness, attuning to changes in daylight and darkness and to changes in vegetation, animal life, and ecosystems in the local area. Celebrating the seasons helps Pagans experience their selfhood as part of the larger realm of nature.

Furthermore, for UU Pagans, celebrating the Sabbats is a powerful way to experience both the seventh Principle, "respect for the interdependent web of all existence of which we are part," and the sixth Source, "spiritual teachings of Earth-centered traditions which celebrate the sacred circle of life and instruct us to live in harmony with the rhythms of nature."

Celebrating seasonal festivals of the Wheel of the Year also builds community among Pagans of many paths and places. Many Pagans share Sabbat greetings, customs, rites, photographs, chants, and other expressions of seasonal celebration with each other face-to-face and in cyberspace through social media, blogs, emails, podcasts, and videos.

Observing Sabbats can also be inspirational, stimulating creative expression and the crafting and sharing of stories, poems, songs, ceremonies, and illustrations, among others. Some Pagans also volunteer and teach about Paganism in public school settings during Sabbat times in order to help dispel common misconceptions about Pagan and Earth-centered religions.

Although Pagans around the world have the Wheel of the Year in common, considerable variety exists in customs and observances. Some focus on symbols and stories rooted in a particular culture, while others take a multicultural approach in creating celebrations. Location is also a factor, as the dates of Sabbats are six months apart in the northern and southern hemispheres. Many Pagans, especially those aligned with Celtic spirituality, begin their Wheel of the Year with the mid-autumn festival of Samhain, the Celtic New Year. Others choose to begin their Wheel of the Year at other festivals, such as the spring equinox or the winter solstice.

Since the renaissance of Paganism in the mid-twentieth century, there has been a growing interest, as well as participation, in celebrating the seasons in Unitarian Universalist congregations, fellowships, churches, and communities across the United States. When a UU Pagan group is part of a congregation, all eight Sabbats of the Pagan Wheel of the

Year are usually observed by the group. Some UU Pagans will also hold personal ceremonies and household festivities. Some UU congregations will observe a Pagan Sabbat with a service on the closest Sunday. Sometimes the service is conducted by one or more UU Pagans, sometimes by a minister or a worship associate, or by a guest minister or other outside speaker.

Five of the eight Pagan Sabbats are among the diverse holidays included on the Unitarian Universalist Association holidays and ceremonies section of its website. The five Sabbats include both solstices, both equinoxes, and Samhain. In addition, the Flower Ceremony that is listed can be adapted to celebrate Beltane. Imbolc and Lughnassadh, although not yet included in this holidays list, are also observed by some.

Over the years, I have conducted Pagan Sabbat Sunday services at a variety of UU congregations across the United States. During these services, I speak to the importance of celebrating seasonal holidays as part of a rich personal and communal spiritual life. In speaking about celebrating the seasons, I emphasize the importance of observing what is happening in the natural world in the locale where the celebration is being held and incorporating those observations in ceremonies. I also share ways to learn about old traditions, including consulting folk sources and adapting them for contemporary celebrations. I also encourage the development of new forms of celebration. It is especially edifying to me to see Pagans crafting new ceremonies, chants, meditations, customs, and other creative ways of celebrating the seasons.

I've included here an overview of the Wheel of the Year as I have worked with it personally, in the Circle Sanctuary Community, and in a variety of Unitarian Universalist communities in the United States.

Samhain, celebrated on or near October 31, is the start and end of the Wheel of the Year. This is the conclusion of the growing season and marks the end of harvest time. Vegetation is dying and humans and animals are preparing for the approaching winter. It is the spiritual new year and a time for contemplation and divination for the coming year. This is a time for remembering and honoring ancestors and loved ones who have died. Some Halloween customs, including wearing costumes, trick-or-treating, and bonfires, have origins in old Samhain traditions.

Winter solstice, celebrated on or near December 21 and also known as Yule, is the start of the new solar year, and heralds the change in the calendar year. It is a time for renewing bonds with family, friends, and community. It is also a sacred time for charitable giving and for praying and working for world peace and a sustainable planet. Yule customs include decorating homes with lights, holly, mistletoe, evergreen wreaths, trees, and sprigs, exchanging gifts, kindling bonfires, burning a yule log, caroling, wassailing, and general revelry.

Imbolc, celebrated on or near February 2, is the festival of waxing light. Also known as Brigid's Day and Candlemas, it celebrates lengthening days with the kindling of candles and other sacred fires. It is sacred to Brigid, Celtic Goddess of poetry, healing, and the forge. As with its secular folk holiday counterpart, Groundhog Day, it is a time for looking for signs of coming Spring. This middle-of-winter holiday was considered the start of Celtic spring in ancient times.

Spring equinox, also known as the vernal equinox and Ostara, is celebrated on or near March 21. This is a celebration of the start of spring and new life. Its symbols of colorful eggs, baskets, and rabbits, sacred to the ancient Germanic goddess Ostara, have been incorporated into many Easter celebrations. Easter derives its name from Eostre, another form of Ostara's name.

Beltane is celebrated on or near May 1. This holiday, also known as May Eve and May Day, is a fertility festival and celebrates the flowering of life. Festivities include Maypole dancing, bonfires, decorating with flowers, and wearing bright colors and head wreaths of flowers and greenery. This festival includes the old folk traditions of selecting and crowning a May Queen and May King and having Morris Dancers awaken the life force in the land with folk dancing. Traditions of honoring mothers with flowers on Mother's Day are said to derive from flower customs connected with this old Celtic holiday, as well as the Floralia, the ancient Roman festival held in honor of the goddess of flowers.

Summer solstice is celebrated on or near June 21 and is also known as Litha, and sometimes by its old name,

Midsummer. This grand gathering time celebrates the longest days of the year and the start of summertime. It is celebrated with community bonfires, singing, dancing, feasting, and all-night revels.

Lughnassadh, also known as Lammas, is celebrated on or near August 1. This holiday celebrates nature's abundant greenery, grain, and the beginning of the harvest. Its customs include celebrating the height of summer with bonfires, feasting, and outdoor games. Country fairs held in many rural areas in July and August continue some of the traditions of this ancient holiday.

Fall equinox, also known as autumn equinox and Mabon, is celebrated on or near September 21. Customs include cider-pressing, canning, and harvest feasts. This is the time of thanksgiving and the celebration of nature's abundance. The cornucopia, also known as the horn of plenty, is a symbol associated with this holiday as with the celebration of Thanksgiving in the United States, which also occurs in November.

I began facilitating seasonal celebrations for others in spring 1971 while a senior at the College of William and Mary in Virginia. The first ceremony I created and led was in my role as president of Eta Sigma Phi, the Classics Honor Society, and the Classics Club. I thought we could celebrate the beauty and joys of springtime as well as enhance our understanding of classical civilizations by enacting a rite of spring. We held our rite on a beautiful April day. We dressed in tunics and togas, and some of us also wore ivy garland crowns on our heads. I led our festival procession of classically garbed professors and students past classroom buildings and dormitories into the Sunken Garden, a beautiful grassy place at the center of the old campus. There we attuned to the beauty of nature and celebrated spring by invoking Dionysus and Gaia. Our re-created Greco-Roman rite of spring was met with good response, not only from those who took part, but also from the many bystanders who delighted in watching us. For me, it was life-changing. It deepened my connection with nature and springtime even more powerfully than my experiences organizing the first Earth Day on campus the previous year. Organizing and leading this ritual marked the beginning of what was to become a lifelong career in creating and facilitating seasonal celebrations that combine old and new ways of connecting with nature.

Forty years later, in October 2011, I revisited the place where my journey first began, and in the autumn of my life, conducted a rite of autumn. This time my rite was sponsored by both the Classics Club and the Unitarian Universalist Circle on campus. This rite, while rooted in Paganism, was multicultural and interfaith, and included not only students and professors, but members of the local community. We celebrated nature and attuned to autumn. With drumming, chanting, and prayers, we affirmed working for a healthier, more sustainable environment and a world with more peace, liberty, and justice for all, intentions that are part of both Unitarian Universalism and Paganism

—and that are fitting to include in every celebration of the seasons.

◄○►

SELENA FOX *is Senior Minister and founder of Circle Sanctuary, an Earth-centered church near Barneveld, Wisconsin, serving Nature spirituality practitioners worldwide since 1974.*

Pagan Depth in Unitarian Universalism: Or, Why UU Polytheism Is Not an Oxymoron

John Beckett

An old joke says that Unitarians believe in one god, at most. Yet some UU Pagans' search for truth and meaning has led us to conclude that there are many gods, each with their own distinct personality, values, virtues, and areas of responsibility.

Like many UU Pagans, I grew up in a very different religion. My family was part of a small fundamentalist Baptist church. They taught that "the saved" (Baptists and a few other fundamentalist Protestants) were going to heaven and everyone else (most Catholics and all non-Christians) was going to hell. At first I believed what I was taught. I had no reason to think the preachers and teachers would tell me something that wasn't the truth, the whole truth, and nothing but the truth.

But when I got to be nine or ten years old, I started thinking about the implications of this theology. Supposedly the Christian God is all-knowing, all-powerful, and all-good: "God is Love." Yet under God's plan the vast majority of the world's population would be condemned to eternal torment for following the wrong religion. What chance does a child born in Saudi Arabia, for example, have of becoming a Christian? If that's God's plan, then it's a pretty lousy plan.

I could not reconcile the idea of infinite punishment for finite sins with the idea of an all-powerful and loving God. About the same time I began to learn about the science of evolution and cosmology. I learned how the Bible was assembled and how the traditionally understood authorship of many of its books is not accepted by many scholars. The foundations of fundamentalism crumbled for me and I became a universalist long before I set foot in a Unitarian Universalist church.

I never seriously considered becoming an atheist. Something inside me kept whispering, "There's more. . . ." Unfortunately, something else inside me kept whispering, "If you're wrong you're going to hell. . . ."

During my young adult years my beliefs could best be described as vague deistic universalism: There is a God and he loves us and will take care of us after we die, but he doesn't really get involved in our day-to-day lives. I attended liberal Christian churches and made some good friends, but there was no real meaning or power in my religion. And that nagging voice from my fundamentalist childhood still whispered, "What if you're wrong?"

That all changed when I met a Wiccan for the first time. Wicca celebrates the divine as female as well as male and finds the divine in nature. This resonated deeply with me. I bought books and magical tools such as wands and chalices, and I started meditating and casting spells. I started celebrating the eight festivals of the Wheel of the Year: the solstices and equinoxes, and the cross quarters in between. It was exciting and interesting. I used words like these in some of the celebrations:

Spirits of the land, Spirits of this place; you who are unseen but felt, unnamed but present; you who were here long before us: we thank you for sharing this place with us. We ask that you join us in celebrating this night, that there might be peace and honor between us. Accept this offering, we ask, given in hospitality, and in love.

But religiously, I had some problems. I could project the Wiccan Goddess onto my concept of the Christian God, but the Horned God (the Wiccan conception of the divine masculine) presented some difficulties. Intellectually I knew he had nothing to do with the Christian devil, but emotionally I wasn't sure. I had no idea what to do with individual gods and goddesses. And the vestiges of fundamentalism were still there, still whispering, "What if you're wrong?"

I dabbled for eight years. I'd buy a Pagan book, try it out, have a little success, run into a complication, then put it down for months at a time. I'd buy a different book, start working through it, come to the section on gods and goddesses, then put it down. I'd realize tonight was the full moon or tomorrow was the summer solstice, throw a ritual together at the last minute and wonder why I didn't feel anything.

Then on Thanksgiving one year, I had an epiphany. A good friend called with questions about ghosts and spirits. I gave him what I thought was a good answer, but the next morning I realized I didn't know what I was talking about. And in that moment I heard a voice. It wasn't audible, but it couldn't have been louder if the Goddess Danu herself had screamed at me from across the table: "GET SERIOUS OR MOVE ON!"

I got serious. I started building a religious foundation. I read liberal Christian books and settled my intellectual understanding of the liberal-fundamentalist debate. I read Buddhist books and learned a very different approach to religious matters. I read history, psychology, and anthropology, and developed a good understanding of the religious impulse.

I started a committed Pagan practice, with meditation, prayers, and devotional observation of nature: going outside and saluting the sun and moon, listening to the birds, touching the Earth, and feeling a part of it all. I discovered Druidry and found that its roots in nature and in Celtic history and culture made it a much better fit for me than Wicca.

After a year of dedicated solitary practice I realized I needed a group. I visited the CUUPS group in Denton,

Texas, and quickly found a home. I started participating in group rituals, and before long I was leading them. The rituals sometimes included words like these:

Morrigan, Battle Raven, Lady of Sovereignty, we ask you to join our circle and bless us with your presence. You who gives the right to rule and who challenges us to rule rightly, be welcome here. Show us our strength, we ask, so we can uphold the Great Work of this time and place.

Morrigan, Queen of Phantoms, Chooser of the Slain, hear us as we call to you. We thank you for your inspiration to stand against those who would rule our lives for their own ends, and to stand against injustice everywhere. Great Queen, let us fight by your side until peace is won. Accept this offering, we ask, given in hospitality, and in love.

The fundamentalist voice in the back of my head was much fainter, but it was still there, still whispering, "But what if you're wrong?"

The next big step on this journey took place as we prepared for our first Egyptian summer solstice ritual in 2004. One of our members had a strong affinity for the gods of ancient Egypt, and so we wanted to do an Egyptian ritual. But we didn't want to do a generic Pagan ritual with Egyptian deities; we wanted to do an actual Egyptian temple ritual. We pored over *The Book of Going Forth by Day* (better known as *The Book of the Dead*), the Coffin Texts, and the Pyramid Texts, all from ancient Egypt. We found academic books and websites that described the daily activities of the priests. We put together a ritual that, while not exactly "authentic," was a good, honest reimagining of ancient Egyptian practices for the twenty-first century. The ritual was a great success, and we've performed an Egyptian summer solstice ritual every year since. It includes these words:

> *Oh water may you remove all evil, as Ra who bathes in the Lake of Rushes. May Horus wash our flesh, may Osiris cleanse our feet, may Shu lift us up and may Nut take our hands.*
>
> *We come before thee, O Isis, O Ra, our purification upon our arms. Assuredly, we are prophets of this temple. We shall not linger, we shall not turn back. We are prophets. We have come to perform the ritual, and we have not come to do that which is not to be done.*

Because this ritual was so different from our usual Wiccan rites and because we had put so much time and effort into creating it, we wanted to do a good job of preparing ourselves to perform it and present it to the public. As part of our preparations we decided to spend nine nights in meditation—one night on each of the gods and goddesses of the Ennead, one of the primary pantheons of ancient Egypt.

I still hadn't given the idea of multiple gods a lot of thought. If you asked, I'd say something like, "All gods are one God and all goddesses are one Goddess." This is soft polytheism—the idea that the many gods and goddesses are aspects or faces of one great God/dess. It's an easy concept for people who live in a monotheistic culture to understand.

But when I got into this series of meditations, I found that my experience of the Sky Goddess Nut was different from my experience of the Earth God Geb. My experience of Isis was different from that of her husband Osiris, and both of those experiences were radically different from my experience of their brother Set. These experiences didn't feel like different faces of one great divine being—they felt like distinctly different beings.

Armed with both personal experience and a wider knowledge of the world's religions, I began to think about the gods again. The great diversity of religious experiences around the world point toward the diversity of the divine. The world as we actually experience it is more easily explained by many gods of limited power and scope than by one all-powerful God. The problem of evil is only the most obvious example. For most of history, much of humanity has honored and worshipped many beings, whether gods and goddesses, ancestors, or nature spirits—and they still do today. Even in supposedly monotheistic religions there are angels, devils, and saints. And how does that whole Trinity thing work anyway? It sure looks like three gods to me.

The final step came one night when in a small-group ritual I had an ecstatic experience of Cernunnos, the god of the animals and the forest. This wasn't a general feeling or an involuntary visualization or a voice in the back of my head. This was ecstatic communion, the distinct presence of a divine being in me. I didn't lose self-awareness like some accounts I've read of divine possession, but I was certain I had another awareness and another will in me. It was amazing, it was powerful, and it was undeniably real. These words were part of our ritual:

> *Cernunnos, Lord of the Animals and Lord of the Hunt, God of the Forest and of Green Growing Things, we ask you to join our circle and bless us with your presence. Great Hunter and Hunted, be welcome here. Teach us what we must learn, so we can join you in the Great Work of this time and place.*

> *Cernunnos, Horned God, God of Nature and Father to our tribe, hear us as we call to you. We thank you for the animals: those that nourish our bodies, those that bring signs and omens, those that inspire us with their beauty and power, and those that accompany us through life. Hunter and Hunted, let us run with you through the forest; teach us again to be wild and free. Accept this offering, we ask, given in hospitality, and in love.*

After this experience, the fundamentalist voice was gone from my head. Intellectually I had rejected it long ago. This let me reject it emotionally as well. I wasn't able to just forget the bad religious experiences of my youth; I had to crowd them out with good experiences of the gods.

I went back and re-read the stories of my ancestors, but I didn't read them like the fundamentalists read the Bible. Instead, I read them looking for hints about how our ancient ancestors lived and how they related to the gods. I contemplated the stories of the gods and meditated on how they could be most meaningful here and now. Most importantly, I studied them to determine the values and virtues of the gods, and found the best way to honor the gods is to embody their virtues and live by their values.

I began to pray to specific gods and goddesses, meditate on them, and make offerings to them. Through consistent ordinary effort, I have come to know the gods better. Good religion is concerned with forming and strengthening relationships: with our families, with our communities, and with the gods who call to us. Regular spiritual practice nurtures my relationships with the gods.

I began to work with other polytheists, some in my CUUPS group and some scattered around the country. We compare experiences, discuss practices, and share scholarship. Polytheism is a minority within the minority of Paganism, and there is a certain collegiality even between followers of gods of widely differing cultures and pantheons.

While in theory it sounds like a terrible mismatch, in practice polytheism works quite well in a Unitarian Universalist setting. Polytheists understand that different people are called to worship different gods—or no gods—in different ways. What an individual believes about the gods is unimportant; what matters is how that person's beliefs cause them to act. Polytheists understand that families and communities exist across many generations. This motivates us to live sustainably so as to leave a better world for future generations. Prayers like this one reflect this understanding:

Ancestors of blood and ancestors of spirit, you whose children we are and on whose foundations we build, because of you we have life. Join our circle, we ask, and add your blessings to this rite. We are your children and grandchildren, and we would hear your wisdom once again. Accept this offering, we ask, given in hospitality, and in love.

Polytheists are reviving and reimagining cultures that were wiped out by the advance of Christianity. This gives us a deep respect for religions, cultures, and people who are oppressed today, and provides us with a profound commitment to social justice.

Ralph Waldo Emerson said, "A man will worship something. . . . That which dominates will determine his life and character. Therefore it behooves us to be careful what we worship, for what we are worshipping we are becoming."

Many in our mainstream society worship mindless consumption and vapid entertainment. Some worship money and power. Many worship their own egos. What are they becoming?

I prefer to worship Cernunnos, the god of the forest, and Danu, the lady of the waters. I prefer to worship Morrigan, the goddess of sovereignty. I prefer to worship Osiris, the lord of the duat, and Isis, the lady of magic.

Ultimately, I don't *know* if there really are many gods of limited scope and power. The true nature of the divine remains as mysterious as ever. But my experiences of the many gods have been meaningful and helpful. Polytheist theology strikes me as a reasonable explanation for the world as we actually experience it. So rather than living in perpetual agnosticism, I order my life as though the gods are real, distinct, individual beings. In honoring them, in living in relationship with them, and in embodying their virtues, I am part of something much larger than myself.

Spirits of the land, spirits of this place; mighty ancestors; Goddesses and Gods; we thank you for your presence and your blessings on our rite and in our lives. May there be peace and honor between us now and forever. Hail and farewell!

⊷⊶

JOHN BECKETT *grew up in Tennessee, where wandering through the woods gave him a sense of connection to nature and a certain Forest God. He is a druid in the Order of Bards, Ovates, and Druids; the coordinating officer of the Denton, Texas, chapter of CUUPS; and a former vice president of CUUPS. His blog "Under the Ancient Oaks" is part of the Pagan Channel of the multifaith website Patheos.*

TOUCHED BY A GODDESS

OM PRAKASH

I have always been a spiritual person—"spiritual but not religious," as some people say now—exploring various paths and looking for some truth that transcended my limited understanding of the world. This is not surprising since I was born in an insular community. The most liberal religions in my neighborhood, near Chester, Pennsylvania, were the Methodists and Lutherans. I didn't know anything about any other faiths except Islam—since the Nation of Islam sold fish and bean pies and pushed the Nation in the area—and the Jehovah's Witnesses, because they proselytized in the community as well.

The Pentecostals and Baptists were most prevalent. Unfortunately, they had a reputation for accusing everyone who was not part of their groups of being lost, deceived, and going to hell. I believed what they told me until I learned more about the larger world. That took a great deal of effort. In our community, we didn't have many opportunities to explore other philosophies and religions because, while ours was an immigrant community with people of many backgrounds, it was still fairly segregated. We all lived there, but we didn't really know each other well enough to discuss religion or politics. Even so, I might have ended up learning quite a bit in that community as I got older, but as the immigrants began to move out because of a downturn in the economy and whites fled urban areas for the suburbs, the neighborhood became more black and more closed off from the white population. This left us more homogeneous and with a narrower religious perspective.

Since my mother was Pentecostal and we were seeking a higher power as a family we constantly heard the Pentecostal message, which some of us explored. The problem was that it left us with only two theological choices—either being Pentecostal, or going to hell. Some of us took the Pentecostal path, some decided on hell. I took both paths, switching back and forth every so often until my late teens, when I became aware of more choices and began to explore spirituality on my own.

This was a change. As children in my household we could never do this. Spiritual experiences were reserved for the people who had been baptized in the Holy Spirit and who were Christian. All others came from Satan, or were the result of trickery come not from God, according to the Pentecostals. So we never talked about alternative spiritual experiences or explored them until we were old enough to leave home, or else we did so in secret. And so some of my deepest exploration took place when I went to college. The first thing I learned about, in a class on speech communication, was the mystical, esoteric practice of dream control—later referred to as "lucid dreaming" by the social scientists who began to study it. The practice consists of realizing that one is dreaming in the midst of the dream and interacting with the world of the dream with the knowledge that it is a dream. I discovered that I was a natural at this. I practiced awakening in my dreams fully conscious and exploring them for several years. I also studied Western philosophy, Eastern philosophy, and psychology.

Reading helped me realize how much I didn't know, and gave me a hunger to learn more. To deal with this lack of knowledge, I created what I called the Triune Theory of Development. This was a step-by-step plan to help me increase my knowledge and mental capacities, increase my physical capacities, and broaden my spiritual understanding through various forms of meditation, with the hope that I would be prepared to receive some type of mystical awakening at the end of my journey.

I stopped reading anything on spirituality and instead engaged in growth and self-improvement for several years, following only my own path and intuition. As a psychology major—and a skeptic—I felt it necessary to avoid being influenced by reading books about other people's spiritual experiences. That way my experiences would be my own and pristine, rather than imagined experiences that matched up with something I read somewhere.

When I was deeply entrenched in the mystical Christian tradition, and as I sought to cast off the Pentecostal tradition in which I had been raised, I came upon something that I found totally shocking and surprising—the revelation of a goddess. I then went into a period of solitary prayer and meditation, praying to have the truth about the universe revealed to me. Revelations about the nature of God came to me several times as mystical experiences and dreams, until one month when I entered into what I describe as a hell-realm. I was living alone in San Diego, working hard, with barely any money. I began to notice all the pain and suffering around me and to identify with it until it was all I could see. I got so sucked into it that I couldn't get out!

I worked alone at night as a security guard making rounds, sometimes under the most beautiful skies I had ever seen. I was crushed, totally depressed. But when I looked up at the brilliant moon surrounded by stars I sensed something there drawing me out of myself. I knew what it was. It was what the Pentecostals had warned me about, something seductive and satanic. Yet, it wasn't. It was warm, beautiful, and alluring. I wanted to connect with that feeling, go deeper, let my feelings of fear and depression wash away and join completely with Her. Somewhere inside I knew it was Her, but I fought for my life, resisting.

I took me time to realize something was wrong. Something was missing—the feeling I had looking at that moon, or experienced in the silence of the night and the peace of the darkness. My depression lifted as I realized that my life choices and my worldview were causing this feeling. That is when I finally decided I needed to change and I left the Pentecostals for a spiritual journey of my own. Back to the Triune Theory, modified.

Memories began to surface, while meditating, from recurring nightmares that I had had as a Pentecostal years before. Other memories surfaced about things that didn't fit while I was Pentecostal—arguing with ministers about how ridiculous the idea of a person going to hell because they weren't Christian; dream control and all that had happened all those years of practicing; a longing for nature and the wonder and beauty of a dark summer-night's moonlit sky. I had really fought these recurring feelings and attractions, especially the latter one, but now I began to follow them.

I continued to experiment in many ways, creating methods myself to explore my spirituality, until one night, as I lay in bed, I had another terrible recurring dream. The original dream was always the same. I could hear something in the dark in my bedroom. I would awaken in the dream and be full of fear. I would reach for the light switch and click it three times, but it wouldn't come on. Something would be moving toward me in the dark. I would strain to see it clearly, but I couldn't. Then I would wake up in terror. The dream was so vivid and real that it left me shaken even after I awoke.

Then one time it was different. I was in the bed like before. I could hear something in the dark. I clicked the light switch. The light came on this time. My father was standing there in the dark and started to speak to me, but he was speaking with a young woman's voice. He was a woman as well as a man. Never before had I allowed myself to connect with the feminine part of the divine.

I was shocked because the feeling there was a feeling of the same presence I had often experienced when meditating but continually tried to ignore—a powerful feminine presence. I had actively fought this all of my life, even as it became more insistent. Somehow it had shifted from a feeling while meditating to an archetypal presence in a dream with its own personality, which was actually aware of me.

The following night as I dreamed I actively decided to pursue this presence. I found it in the form of a beautiful woman full of golden light standing in front of my childhood home. It seemed that the energy of the universe was cycling through her. She was like a diamond, the most beautiful thing I have ever seen, like a golden jewel. She was so beautiful that I can't even see the image in my mind's eye. There was a low, roaring sound like the crackling fire of a furnace filling her with golden light. As I approached her she looked at me and smiled as if she knew me. I realized that I did know her. I had known her forever.

We walked toward each other and touched, palm to palm. I could feel energy running up from the base of my spine all the way to crown of my head and then there was a loud, high-pitched sound as the top of my head opened and energy poured upward. I awakened and sat up in my bed with the energy still flowing upward for several minutes, connecting me with everything in the universe. When it stopped I found that I was still connected and have been ever since.

I needed a place to talk about this experience, but I didn't have one anywhere. Since I hadn't studied anything or read books about what I was experiencing, it was a total mystery, even though I knew something had happened. I could still feel the effects. A friend of mine who studied Hinduism and had dabbled in Paganism told me that I had had a *kundalini* experience. He also told me that the woman I had seen, who called herself Diana, was a Pagan goddess. He gave me Sri Chinmoy's book *Kundalini: The Mother-Power*. I discovered that I had been doing meditations like the ones outlined in the book, and the power that I experienced was that of the divine feminine, the Goddess—something that I had avoided exploring all of my life because of fear. But now I had to explore it. I didn't know where, until I remembered this strange religion called Unitarian Universalism.

A Baptist missionary had once told me that he didn't accept Unitarian Universalists because they were crazy and didn't know what they believed. He had been wrong about everything else he told me, so I decided he might be wrong about Unitarian Universalists too. This experience gave me the opportunity to finally explore the Unitarian Universalist church. He was wrong again, of course, because I loved it when I got there.

I came into the church quite nervous, since I had given up on most churches. There were also very few people of color. It was summer so the services were being led by members of the congregation, many of whom were mystical naturalists and Pagans. I loved the place. Something about it just connected with me. When the minister returned I connected with her as well. She began to help me get the right books and connect with the right people to explore my strange dream and newfound spirituality.

I will not pretend everything was perfect. Many doors opened, but many were slammed in my face. As in many other groups and communities, there were some who were very open. Others, as members of a traditionally oppressed community (i.e., Pagans) had serious, unresolved issues when it came to my gender, race, and history. They had issues with each other, too. I found it impossible to work with the ones who chose to engage in dysfunctional behavior since I wasn't willing to go there. Despite their issues and the combative behavior of a minority of the congregation, I found my place in the UU world and was involved with the Covenant of Unitarian Universalist Pagans for several years. During that time my spiritual beliefs expanded.

I began to explore Hinduism, Buddhism, and other spiritual practices. I reclaimed a more realistic view of Christianity: mystical Christianity, which included the divine feminine. I explored wisdom traditions and Yogic philosophy. None of this would have been possible without the openness, acceptance, and support of the Unitarian Universalist mystical naturalist and Pagan community. Many, many people welcomed me wholeheartedly for who I was, not for what I had been. I wasn't that surprised by this acceptance because of an incident that occurred when I first joined the Unitarian Society of Germantown in Philadelphia.

After I joined, I and two other new members were invited to be part of a service and share our odysseys. I nervously spoke about my spiritual journey for the first time, and my connection with the beautiful, golden figure. When I finished I received a standing ovation instead of ridicule. Since that time, when it comes to sharing and being part of a community, I have learned to hear the applause and enjoy the acceptance, to draw close to those who can share that experience, and to let the others go. Through many dangers, toils, and snares I have finally learned to draw close to the acceptance and eschew the ridicule, which is one of the most important lessons that I could have learned.

The Goddess and I are still connected. We have been involved in a great spiritual journey throughout the years, and that is something I don't see changing soon. Singing, moving meditation, and chanting often connect me to Her in all of her forms. Not only to Her, but to every tree, every flower, every person on this planet, Mother Earth. To me, She became the Beloved, moving the wheel of time.

—◇—

OM PRAKASH (JOHN GILMORE) *is a massage therapist, workshop leader, and life coach specializing in reinventing work and spirituality. He has written several books and articles on practical spirituality and using belief systems to enhance lives and build communities. He is now retired from the ministry after serving as a Unitarian Universalist minister for more than fifteen years.*

Born of Earth

Jan Ögren

Growing up Unitarian Universalist, I wasn't entirely sure what I was, but I knew what I wasn't. I wasn't irrational: I didn't believe something just because someone told me it was true. I wasn't following a faith because others believed it. I wasn't trying to convert anyone to my religion, which was fortunate, because I wasn't quite sure what my religion was.

I knew Unitarian Universalism had a lot to do with social justice and equal rights. In 1965, my mother responded to Martin Luther King Jr.'s call for help and joined hundreds of other Unitarian Universalists to march to Montgomery, Alabama. She told me about the murder of Viola Liuzzo, another UU mother who marched that day with her. I was proud of her, and proud to be part of a religion where people were brave enough to act in accordance with their principles. But I wasn't sure what being a Unitarian Universalist really meant.

I knew I was supposed to search for truth and meaning (our fourth Principle), and that the first Source of that knowing was direct experience. The only problem was that my direct experience of the world seemed quite different from that of other people. I first realized this when I was five years old and playing tag with the neighborhood children. We were using a young elm tree for our home base. A boy made a dash for the tree to avoid my friend Sara, who was "it." He laughed as he stood safely under its shade. Reaching up into the tree, he casually ripped off a branch, swung it around a few times, and then tossed the branch aside. I stood there immobile with shock. Sara took advantage of my confusion and ran up to me. "You're it!" she yelled, tapping me on the head. All the kids ran off shouting with joy, leaving me alone with the tree. My right arm throbbed with a deep pain as I looked at it. There was a jagged scar on the trunk, where the tree had tried desperately to hold onto its limb.

I didn't care about the game anymore. With tears streaming down my face, I went searching for my mom. She assured me the tree would be okay and that my dad would seal off the wound so that it could grow new branches. I'd watched my dad carefully pruning our trees in a respectful manner, so I knew that he could heal the tree. What worried me was the undeniable fact that I was fundamentally different from my peers. It was as impossible for me to rip a branch off a tree as it was to cut off my own hand. Yet I'd watched the other kids laughing as the boy broke the branch.

Not only was I connected to plants, but I also had a special sense about the weather. My dad had a similar weather-knowing, which reassured me that it was "normal," or at least that it was okay to be different in this way. People called him lucky because he had beautiful sunny days for hikes, picnics, and special events, and he knew to plan something indoors for days that would be rainy. Using direct experience and the Unitarian Universalist value of rationality, I began testing my knowing about the weather. I'd write down my prediction, based on an inner sense I couldn't name, before checking on the weather service's advice. Then I would see who was more accurate. Like my father, my forecast was much more reliable than the newspaper's.

When I was twelve years old my best friend was Basil, our black-and-white cat. I would watch him and try to figure out how he knew certain things, like when someone was going into the kitchen or when his buddy, the neighbor cat, was outside. Around that same time, my older brother was practicing Transcendental Meditation. My mom told me it was to help him be less angry, but the way he'd scream at me if I made too much noise while he was meditating didn't give me much faith in its success. It did give me the idea that maybe that's what Basil was doing when he sat on the end of my bed: paws tucked neatly underneath his chest, eyes closed, head up. People said he was sleeping, but I'd observed him fall asleep once in that position. His head had slowly drooped until his nose hit the blanket, then he jerked his head back up and seemed to return to what I assumed was a meditative state.

Lying next to him on the bed, I tried to sense what he was experiencing. Over time, I began to feel his presence when we meditated together. I started seeing images of the world as though my geometry homework was superimposed over the landscape. Lines extended from the sides of buildings, continuing beyond the walls and into space where they intersected with lines stretching from other buildings, trees, and roads. People moved through these lines, setting off vibrations like the playing of a stringed instrument. I started to sense the world as Basil did; I also had this sense of where people were in relation to me. I found this very helpful because it allowed me to "see" my mother coming home, so that by the time she opened the door I had my dishes in the sink and the rock-and-roll music turned down low.

I was very thankful that I wasn't raised with the negative Christian view of cats and witches, and that I didn't hold any beliefs in devils or hell. I was relieved that I didn't have the fears and guilt that some of my friends suffered while being raised Jewish or Christian, but I still longed for a deeper understanding of the world. My parents' Humanism offered me guidance and an ethical foundation for acting in the world, but not for understanding the spiritual nature of reality. So when I got to college, I went exploring. I tried Hinduism, which in the 1970s meant hanging out with the Hari Krishnas. Chanting with them allowed me to shut off my rational mind, which enabled me to feel peace and love in a way I'd never felt before. This filled me with both joy and fear, as I didn't want to stray too far from Unitarian Universalist values and become irrational. Zen Buddhism gave me a way to still my mind without chanting, but it was focused too much on humans and not enough on nature. Judaism had the amazing Kabbalah wisdom, which felt overwhelming and far beyond my ability to comprehend. While studying with a Christian mystic, I had an experience of becoming one with everything. I had trouble integrating that experience into my life, however, and the Christian God was too small to explain what I felt, since at that time I still held a limited view of Christianity.

I gained some wisdom from all of these faiths, but still the only one who'd taught me something I could fully embrace was my cat, Basil. My studies earned me a degree in psychology and religion and a concern that maybe something was truly wrong with me, because I hadn't managed to fit into any of the religions I'd studied. I was terrified that all the experiences I'd had with nature and animals might be the product of hallucinations and that I might actually be insane. My desperate search to understand what was normal and abnormal eventually led me to a job working with schizophrenics at a state mental hospital. There I met another psychiatric technician, Red Eagle, who was a Mescalero Apache medicine man. He'd been raised by his grandfather on the reservation, where talking to spirits was accepted and encouraged.

I began apprenticing with him, and the first thing he did was perform a dedication ceremony for me. This is usually done for an infant a few days after they're born. I was twenty-two years old when I was finally formally introduced to the world. Before the ceremony, I'd felt like a foreigner at a cocktail party where I didn't know the people or the language. I'd stand on the sidelines, awkwardly pretending to be what I assumed others wanted me to be. Then Red Eagle introduced me to my Mother Earth and Father Sun, who gave me life and energy. I met my brothers and sisters, the winds, and realized that they were the ones who informed me about the weather. With Red Eagle's help, I discovered that I was related to all beings—and for the first time in my life, I felt I belonged in this world.

As my studies in the Mescalero Apache medicine way deepened, I learned to hear spirits more clearly. It was like expanding my circle of friends. Red Eagle would laugh at Westerners who were so enthralled with them that they would believe whatever the spirit said. "Treat spirits like any other friend," he advised me. "If they give helpful advice, follow it. But always listen to yourself first." This fit exactly with what my Unitarian Universalist upbringing had taught me: to use direct experience and my rational mind to determine my course in life.

A Pueblo medicine man taught me a song to use while driving to ask the stoplights to turn green. As a good scientist, I counted the number of stoplights that were red when I didn't sing the song, and the number of red lights when

I did sing. After years of these tests, it was clear that the stoplights enjoyed being sung to. It was also an extremely practical skill, because I have a habit of running late for events, and this helps me arrive on time.

In Red Eagle's view of the world, he was teaching me a way of life, not a religion. It wasn't about believing in things as much as connecting to the amazing world around me. He explained that the different religions were like spokes in a wheel leading to the center, and that there were many ways of coming home to that sense of connection with all beings. He believed Native Americans were at the center of the wheel, where all the different religions met. That also described Universalism in a way that made sense to me. I finally had answers for when people asked me about Unitarian Universalism and what I believed.

When I talk with Unitarian Universalist youth, I often hear the familiar lament of how difficult it is to explain Unitarian Universalism. "When people ask you what your religion is, tell them you're a Universalist," I recommend. "It's easier for people to understand because *Universal* is a word they can relate to: like universal love, or being part of the universe. Around the world there are many different religions, but at the center is Universalism."

People often ask me about my spiritual experiences and my ability to talk with guides. A Unitarian Universalist mother once shared that when her son was very young he said that he had a visitor who came to his room every night. Not knowing how to respond, she smiled and left him to deal with it. Later she read about how common it was for children to have spirit guides. She asked her son, now an adult, what had happened to the visitor. He told her that he could tell she was uncomfortable with his visitor, so he told him to go away and he never saw him again.

After hearing that story, I began looking for opportunities to share about my childhood experiences of sensing and seeing things differently. I wanted parents to feel comfortable encouraging their children to experience the fullness of the magical world we live in. After telling my stories over and over again, my spirit guides suggested that I write a novel. I responded that I couldn't. I wasn't an "author." But they insisted. They even promised to help market the book once I'd written it.

So I wrote *Dividing Worlds*, a story about Miranda, a young woman who just wants to lead a normal life—but there are spirits who need her help. The cave they've been guarding for centuries is now buried under a pharmaceutical company's manufacturing plant. With the assistance of an extinct bear, a mystical cat, an Irish ghost, and a law student, Miranda attempts to help the spirits while trying not to jeopardize her job or ruin her relationship. Everything in the book is based on my or other people's actual experiences. Because Miranda is loosely based on me, she is of course a Unitarian Universalist. That allowed me to write a book about a UU shaman as a way of validating for myself and others that it's perfectly logical and normal to be a Unitarian Universalist and a mystic.

The spirits kept their side of the bargain related to marketing, and in 2015, *Dividing Worlds* was translated into Portuguese and published in Brazil. I'll be curious to learn if the UU Church of the Larger Fellowship will start receiving requests for information about Unitarian Universalism from people in Brazil.

Stories are a wonderful way to learn about something new. Red Eagle often taught by telling tales about how he grew up on the reservation. Sometimes animals and spirits tell me stories, which I write down. I've shared many of them at UU congregations when they have a "Story for All Ages" as part of the Sunday service. I gathered twelve of them together in a book called *Dragon Magic: Amazing Fables for All Ages*.

I used to be nervous about sharing my mystical side with other Unitarian Universalists. I was afraid I'd be considered one of *those* people—the irrational ones. But my experiences are all firmly based in direct experience and tested, using my scientifically based rational mind. Prior to meeting Red Eagle, I discovered the Institute of Noetic Sciences (IONS), where they study consciousness. There scientists explore telepathy, energy healing, and everything else I'm curious about. My connection to IONS helped balance my shamanistic apprenticeship with my love of science, and it reassured me that others were not only stepping into the mystical world, but they were also analyzing it and proving it to be real.

When I share about who I am, I try to be as brave as my mother was when she traveled to Montgomery, Alabama, to stand up for her faith. So now, when asked, I say, "I'm a UU Shaman." Having found my center, I can more fully embrace being a Unitarian Universalist, which expresses all of the wisdom of Humanism, Hinduism, Buddhism, Judaism, Christianity, Paganism, and more. Red Eagle showed me the center of the wheel where all of these religious paths meet, that universal space where all life resides.

◄○►

JAN ÖGREN *is a lifelong Unitarian Universalist, an international author, a public speaker, a licensed psychotherapist, and a medicine woman. Her novel* Dividing Worlds *features a UU protagonist who is trying to save the world. She writes UU fables for all ages and is a guest speaker at many UU congregations. Her most recent book,* Dragon Magic: Amazing Fables for All Ages, *was published in 2015 (*www.JanOgren.net*).*

Neo-Transcendentalists

Amy Beltaine

I sped across sunbaked Montana, alone, in a beat-up Buick Skyhawk, heading east. I love the high desert plateau. Sagebrush country reminds me of all the backpacking trips I took with my dad, watching him gleefully breathe in the scent of sagebrush. He stood so still, I swear he was listening to the rocks shimmer in the sun. I glanced in the rearview, and had to look again. Gold and orange and pink streaked the sky behind me, demanding my full attention. I parked, emerged from my steel cocoon into the dry heat, and gingerly propped myself against the trunk. As the sun sank lower, pink transformed to red, lavender to purple: a surround-sound symphony of color. Reflected in my body's memory were sunsets on the Oregon coast, Mom singing out, "Oh, just look at those colors!" It was time to drop everything and worship at the altar of Mother Earth.

Followers of Earth-centered traditions frequently sing a traditional Hopi chant with the words,

The Earth is our Mother
We must take care of her.

We are called to explore what it might mean to be in respectful relationship with our whole Earth: human, plant, mineral, and animal alike. How might we worship this sacred source with our hearts and with our hands? Paganism is about what we do, more than what we believe.

My spiritual tree has mystic roots and three main branches. The roots take nourishment from nature and music. The three branches bloom with the wisdom of feminist theology, process theology, and religious naturalism. Feminist theology: We are created by our relationships, and those relationships are sacred. Process theology: We are constantly in change, unfolding; the world tends toward complexity and diversity, which should be celebrated. Religious naturalism: Our world, from stars to stones, contains our sacred story and carries solace, strength, and deep meaning.

In moments of pain and loss I imagine the universe enfolding me in its arms.

As I studied for the Unitarian Universalist ministry I was warned by ministers and association leaders to keep my Earth-based spirituality and practices quiet. Luckily, the reactionary responses to spirituality in general and Pagan traditions in particular are falling away as Unitarian Universalism matures.

I am firmly within the Earth-based circle, and in some ways, so are we all. Have you ever said "knock on wood"?

Wood, from the living tree. Trees have been the dwelling place of spirits, and have been revered in many cultures. The tree of life shows up in religions all over the world. That tree is on the cover of an earlier version of the Unitarian Universalist hymnal. Do you carry a worry stone, a shell, or a gold ring? These Earthy things comfort and connect you to what matters. How very Pagan!

Earth-relating spiritualities evoke ancient human spiritual exploration. They speak to the needs of many. Pagan communities are created through covenant, a promise to participate and to adhere to the ethics inherent in our view of divinity. We worship like our ancestors did twenty thousand years ago, *and* we create ritual and meaning anew. We sing "We Are an Old People" by Morning Feather:

We are the old people
We are the new people
We are the same people
Stronger than before

As president of the Covenant of Unitarian Universalist Pagans, I have spoken with hundreds of UU Pagans and Earth-relating Unitarian Universalists. Some are practitioners of a revived, reconstructed, or newly created movement or faith with lineage, elders, ceremonies, and shared beliefs. Some are fierce defenders of our ecosystems, the Earth, our home. Some connect with family or cultural legacies of sacred place or tribe. Some have joyfully found affirmation through the divine feminine. Some are religious, spiritual, or both—or neither. Some nurture their souls simply by spending time in nature.

For Earth-relating spiritualities, song and ritual hold a central place. On sacred days, the changes of the seasons, or at rites of passage, we gather for worship and ritual.

Common to both Unitarian Universalists and Pagans are rituals to evoke sacred space. In our UU congregations we light the chalice and speak opening words. This ritual helps us to set the chatter of the everyday aside and to be fully present in the moment. Many Pagans refer to this moment in worship as *casting the circle*.

Some of our American Unitarian forebears, especially Transcendentalists like Ralph Waldo Emerson, believed awe to be more important than reason, creativity more important than theory, action more important than contemplation, and the artist to be the epitome of civilization. You could call UU Pagans neo-Transcendentalists.

We need the richness of myth and poetry and a sense of connection with ourselves and the universe that Earth-relating spirituality offers. These include, and reach beyond, the vocabularies of reason and intellect. They evoke the playful self and invite the wise inner knowing of the body to join our rational minds so that our whole selves are present. This larger or "trans-rational" way of experiencing the world is not to be confused with the romantic idea of the "noble savage" or innocent paradise lost. In fact, much of the antipathy toward Earth-centered spirituality and Pagans among Unitarian Universalists can be blamed on a confusion between pre-rational and holistic knowing.

Delight in the mystical, nature, play, non-rational knowing, and ancient wisdom should not be misunderstood as a return to childish things or a rejection of science. Rather, these augment our scientific knowing. The Transcendentalists walked that same middle path. Theirs was an organic response to the Unitarian emphasis on intellectual reason. They longed for a more intense spiritual experience than what was offered by the calm rationalism of the Unitarians. They drew on the ideas of the Romantics without leaving behind empirical science. We sing an elemental chant:

Earth my body, water my blood
Air my breath and fire my spirit

The divine is within us and surrounds us—an immanent and intimate concept of divinity. We do not worship trees or rocks. We revere the divine presence contained within everything. As Shakespeare wrote in *As You Like It*: "And this our life, exempt from public haunt, / Finds tongues in trees, books in the running brooks, / Sermons in stones, and good in everything."

Earth demands your attention. It often provides opportunities for spiritual experiences. Perhaps it was when you pulled a weed and were enveloped by the Earthy smell of freshly disturbed soil or when you inhaled the salty tang of the ocean. Maybe it was when you looked up and were stunned by a shining snow-capped mountain. These experiences can be described by cold hard facts: photons, H_2O, and olfactory function. Yet sometimes facts are inadequate. The awe and wonder, the sense of being transported beyond yourself, or of touching an awareness of the divine, is a spiritual experience.

That experience is direct, personal, and physical. Pagans and Unitarian Universalists trust direct experience as the most important way of developing spiritual knowledge. Earth-relating spirituality invites us to include our bodies in our spiritual experience. Therapists have discovered in the past few decades that all that talk therapy isn't enough. Now, therapy also involves the somatic or embodied experience. We are physical creatures. Everything we experience, we experience through our senses. We feel the Earth under our feet. However, most of us grew up disembodied; our only awareness was of our imperfection, and our inner knowing starved.

What joy and richness is available to us if we cultivate an awareness of our own physical selves? I suffered in high school: I was fat, short, and shy. Then I discovered ancient and indigenous traditions that celebrated bodies. Neolithic depictions of the Goddess were unambiguously fat and yet divine. Modern Pagan ritual explicitly told me, "You are divine." I slowly shed body-shame and began to celebrate myself.

The Transcendentalists believed that humans were inherently good, and that nature was good. Modern Pagans put those two truths together and added it up to being body-positive. What a freeing idea: my body is good, your body is good, our bodies are *meant* to be enjoyed! Eco-feminist theologian Starhawk, in her rendition of "The Charge of the Goddess," reminds us of the sacred ritual words attributed to the Star Goddess: "Let My worship be in the heart that rejoices, for behold, all acts of love and pleasure are My rituals."

Most Pagans are pantheistic or polytheistic. Both are grounded in the belief that divinity can manifest in many ways. Some of us prefer the word *panentheistic*: the divine is many and one, within all and beyond all at the same time. This is similar to how Unitarian Universalists embrace theological diversity. Among the Pagans I know there are deists, theists, Humanists, Unitarian Universalists, Methodists, Muslims, Quakers, and Episcopalians. Some say that the goddesses and gods are ethereal energy forms. Others call them symbols, powers, archetypes, or something deep and strong within the self. Still others describe the divine as something akin to the force of poetry and art. For most, everything is holy. Everything.

The maiden, mother, and crone are all divine images. So is the Infant God, the Hunter God, and the Green Man.

When I eat ice cream I'm aware of the divinity in the cream, the animal that gave the milk, the people who transported it, the spoon with the metals that came from the Earth and were forged with heat and skill, and the bowl, made by my stepfather in his pottery studio. I am, as essayist E. B. White put it, torn between savoring the world and saving it. That reverence and love for our world is a deep motivator to serve life and to save what we can.

Henry David Thoreau, another foundational Transcendentalist, wrote with love about the land and nature and his connection with the seasonal cycles, in defense of the Earth that was his home. I resonate with his words, and yearn for the opportunity to also retreat to a cabin in the woods. But then, my modern self, who is married to a student of natural resource management, says: "Even if we all could retreat to cabins in the woods, we would still be unsustainably impacting our world, instead of making it a better place." I see UU Pagans finding inspiration in Thoreau, but I'm thrilled to see us taking that love of nature one step further: We are learning from science, and committing ourselves to learning and living in harmony with the Earth, to the best of our abilities.

In Earth-relating spirituality the Earth is visualized as a living organism, whom some call Gaia. Gaia is an immense *process*. Gaia is a being made up of other beings. Gaia is us, searching for more justice and more love. Gaia is us, supporting each other in our quests for truth and meaning. The divine is yet larger. My favorite image of the divine is of a loving, human-shaped, star-studded, universe holding the Earth in its embrace. We sing the chant "She Changes Everything She Touches" by Starhawk:

> *She changes everything she touches*
> *And everything she touches changes.*

The Pagan tradition called Wicca has a moral code called the Rede: "An' it harm none, do what you will." Almost all traditions share the acceptance that we are connected to, and therefore responsible for, our fellow creatures: "Do no harm." That's a very high standard!

This is in opposition to the Pagans of popular imagination, with evil witches, devil worshippers, and the old green-faced hag. Or the racist associations of indigenous religions with cannibalism, Voodoo dolls, and screaming savages. Fear of the other may play well on the big screen, but it dehumanizes and strips the sacred out of the world. Earth-based stories and myths have a different message: a story of oneness and connection.

The bad press reminds me of the stories that were made up about early Universalists. Their opponents thought that without punishment in hell people would get up to all sorts of bad behavior. Like the historical Universalists, Pagans are motivated to care for one another and our world because we know that we are loved and lovable.

There are many Pagan views of the afterlife, such as reincarnation and a heavenly place called the "Summerland," but like Unitarian Universalists we are motivated to build the world we dream about in the here and now.

Earth-relating spirituality comes in lots of flavors and forms: indigenous traditions, family traditions, reconstructions, and new religious groups and movements. Mystics throughout history have sounded like Earth-based practitioners. Hildegard of Bingen described God as *viriditas*, which means to me: rich and green and juicy! Drawing the circle of Earth-relating people wider, I include scientists and Humanists, cosmologists and ecologists.

It all comes together for me in the image of the universe enfolding the Earth in its arms. The sacredness of the whole universe and the interdependence of everything.

I draw my circle of faith broadly. My faith is framed by the words that I found in the Bible growing up and grounded in Earth-relating spiritualities. I am aligned with Buddhism and inspired by process and womanist celebration of our interdependent existence. As Walt Whitman mused, "Do I contradict myself? Very well then I contradict myself, (I am large, I contain multitudes)."

―◦―

AMY BELTAINE *is the sole proprietor of Listen to HeartSong. She is affiliated with Atkinson Memorial Church in Oregon City and is president of the board of CUUPS. She supports the League of Women Voters of Portland in their office half-time and spends the rest of her professional time preaching, teaching, coaching, and mentoring.*

Taking a Stand

Wesley Hildebrand

Unitarian Universalism has taught me to question and challenge the status quo set for us by the standards of our society and government. This is reflected in my everyday life as a college student just starting to take my place in the world to try to make a difference. A key principle I learned as a Unitarian Universalist is inclusivity and equality for all living beings. For me as a Pagan, this means all that is living. This principle is reflected in my work as an environmental activist. My Pagan heart and roots hold tightly my love for a healthy Earth. The Earth is my church and my home. My being is called to be a force for changing the systems we use today that are destroying our environment and planet.

Unitarian Universalism has taught me to honor the Earth as sacred and important. Growing up as a Pagan in a UU environment has taught me to respect the Earth, which is my home, my life, my Goddess. I grew up being surrounded by nature and being taught that everything living is intertwined,

leading me to believe that one small change leads to many
other changes. I like to use the butterfly effect as an example
of this. It reflects the theory that if a butterfly flaps its wings,
that little gust of wind could eventually build up into a
storm somewhere else in the world. I see the possibility of
who I am as a young adult in today's world as that butterfly.
My actions have an impact on everything else in the world.

I have learned to question society's status quo around
the environment. Many Unitarian Universalists and Pagans
have very environmentally aware approaches to gathering
and taking from the Earth. However, mainstream America
tends to "do now, think later" regarding the consequences
of activities with potential environmental impact. I have
learned from my beliefs to think critically about all aspects
of my actions and their environmental effects. Many
humans take the environment for granted. I bring questions to those who do not honor our planet. I am becoming
knowledgeable about where our resources, such as food,
water, and other essentials for life are gathered. I stand
up to educate and challenge the misuse of our resources.

Being an environmentally aware activist causes me to
challenge the status quo. I look to educate people who do
not question the consequences of defacing the Earth for
resources and who contaminate the Earth's atmosphere,
land, and water. As a UU Pagan environmental activist, my
upbringing trained me to think critically and to consider all
the results my actions could bring about—what happens
when I throw things away, how I eat, how I care for my

elders, and how the holy exists for me. This critical stance is becoming more prevalent in young adults in the United States. We have wisdom to share. Much of our society has a very subjugating view toward the environment. But what if we stopped and listened to the environment as a living organism? What if we honored what it is telling us? For many, this sounds like heresy. But I think we need heretics to buck these systems if we are to survive.

For me, the status quo surrounding how we treat the environment goes against my Unitarian Universalist and Pagan beliefs of listening to the Earth, caring for it as my home, honoring it as a temple, and conserving and protecting it as I would any human I hold dear.

It is important to me that we assess and stop clear-cutting forests and destroying habitats that have been evolving for thousands of years. This harms the natural environment that has been worked and reworked to perfection by the Earth for millennia. I want to see us stop mining—whether it be strip mining, pit mining, or deep-tunnel mining. This impacts and hurts the surface of the Earth and makes the area useless, defacing the Goddess that is our planet.

We ignore the signs Mother Earth is giving to us, warning us of the destruction we are causing to the environment. Most importantly, I suggest that the human race as a whole does not live in a sustainable manner, that we take more from the Earth than we can afford. I wonder if there will even be resources left for future generations.

As one human being, I believe I can affect the discourse of people not taking care of the planet by "walking my talk." I can influence it by talking about the problem in a manner that other people can hear, and that also addresses the problems without blaming anyone. I can be a leader who empowers people to take action. I can pursue a career where I can influence the media to start addressing what is really going on with our environment.

I can talk to my circle of close friends and family about what they can do to make a difference. I can start a butterfly effect that influences thousands of people, if not more. To do this I need to train myself to speak about the large issues in a way that will affect the prevailing discourse. There are many different opinions about how the environmental situation should be handled. Being a Unitarian Universalist has taught me to see the varying discourses clearly. Unitarian Universalists and Pagans too frequently operate out of a scarcity mentality and not enough from abundance thinking. We tend to take flak from larger religions and let them convince us that these issues are too big for us to make a difference.

I have learned, however, that if I—if we—get out of our own way, stop thinking we are alone and have to handle it all, we can move mountains. This is a lesson I learned when I became an Eagle Scout, as a Unitarian Universalist and a Pagan, building an outdoor classroom in which to teach elementary-age children. My two religions had turned away from Scouting or even banned it outright in their places of worship because of the national organization's views on social issues, instead of looking for solutions and shifting the conversation from within. I had to learn to communicate my take on God and country, as someone who holds the Goddess as sacred and believes that a country's boundaries are one of the leading factors in the current environmental crisis. It was challenging, but I rose up to the challenge needed to move forward to become an Eagle Scout. Even so, I went against the status quo of what my faith communities told me about an organization that I knew had made a difference in my life, an organization that trained me to work with the Earth, recognize her heart, and listen to the trails, forests, and beings around me.

I am a young man who just believes in walking my talk. I do small things, which have a small impact on their own, but have a large impact when done collectively. I participate in larger actions, like helping the university I attend work to divest from fossil fuels. With my parents, I work to make our home more energy efficient and environmentally friendly by composting, growing our own food, switching to LED light bulbs, and installing windows with better insulation.

As I have done all of this I am moved to work to expand and take on larger projects to create a society that cares for its home. I attended the Parliament of the World's Religions in 2015 to network and meet other people working toward the same goal. This is a gathering of people working together as a world community, all driven by different reasons, different religious and spiritual paths, to take on the issues of our time. Many peace leaders, environmentalists, and religious figures from around the world were there. By attending, I allowed myself the opportunity to interact with them. I was able to hear their opinions and engage in dialogue, so these people of influence were able to hear me, too.

I hope that Unitarian Universalism will continue to support Pagan or Earth-and-nature-centered thinkers for the future. As Unitarian Universalist Pagans, we hear our Earth. We listen to her. We can teach others to do this. Just as the Unitarian Universalist faith teaches us to learn and gather our spiritual influences from the many different faiths, I hope my love, our love, of the Earth as Pagans will be that butterfly in the world of religion. My vision is that our Pagan voices honoring our planet will blend together with the voices of those embracing the mysteries of science through logic, and that we will stand together to save our planet. It is here I stand.

-◄o►-

WESLEY HILDEBRAND *is a student at Salem State University in Massachusetts. He achieved the rank of Eagle Scout in the Boy Scouts. Thanks to his faith as a Unitarian Universalist Pagan and with the leadership skills he acquired during his work with the Boy Scouts of America, he feels guided to move forward to change the systems of the world that he sees are not accepting of others.*

Finding Resolve in Liturgical Dilemmas

Kendyl L. R. Gibbons

The roots of my peculiarly Unitarian Universalist Pagan inclination most likely originate in a duck pond. Growing up in a 1950s-era Washington, DC, Unitarian fellowship, of which my parents were all but founding members, I had no home church building until I was in my early teens. Various temporary rental quarters served our congregation during my grade-school years, but one constant throughout that time was a periodic field trip to a local cemetery. In the middle of it lay a large ornamental pond framed in weeping willows, complete with a small picturesque island accessed over a bridge of vaguely oriental design. The pond was occupied by a flotilla of what seem in retrospect impossibly white, fat, complacent ducks, who accepted our tribute of bread crumbs with graceful dignity. As far as I can recall, no one ever articulated to us the significance of this cultivated loveliness surrounded on all sides by the resting dead, but

I was aware of something important in this juxtaposition: a meaningfulness held in vibrant balance that neither the graves nor the ducks would have had alone.

I am confident that neither my parents nor Sunday-school teachers set out to raise a liturgical Pagan, yet that was the option that their influence left most accessible to me by the time they were done. Let it be noted that intellectually, I remain a thoroughgoing Humanist, to whom the concept of a supernatural deity of any sort, or any number, has never made any sense or felt at all compelling. Nevertheless, the roots of a naturalistic mysticism were planted by the program that my UU Sunday school orchestrated and my parents endorsed, in the service of an ascetic spiritual minimalism. The experience of reverence was designed to have its locus in three paradigmatic events. I do not so much remember these as experiences in my own life as I recall the expectation from the adults that these events happen to each of us at some point, and that we would attach the word *wonder* to them. One was finding a dead bird in the backyard—the curriculum assumed that all children had suburban backyards (as well as mothers, fathers, and all the other accoutrements of mid-century middle-class America). Another was planting a bean seed in a Dixie cup at Sunday school and seeing it sprout (after which the nascent plant usually died of neglect). The third was the annual spring ritual of flower communion.

My spiritual journey as a born-and-raised Unitarian Universalist might best be described as a reverse commute. My parents treated the paternal god of their own unsatisfying Midwest-American Protestant heritage as an intellectual disability, something to be overcome if a person had the capacity, and to be treated with respectful sympathy if they did not. I grew into my own inchoate inner life of spiritual awareness in much the same way that my more religiously conventional peers were left to discover their sexuality—without guidance or vocabulary, in secrecy and baffled embarrassment, moved by tides of inexorable experience too powerful to be ignored. The only place my religious community had ever offered to me as a holding environment for that spiritual impulse was the natural world.

The other resource that UU religious education provided was an appreciative familiarity with the myth narratives of various cultures. I now suspect that the agenda behind the book and curriculum *From Long Ago and Many Lands*, with its plethora of creation stories and other tales of the origins of things, was to relativize the Judeo-Christian narratives by presenting them as equals among many such stories—a perspective that I appreciate, and that has served me well. Our iconic Christmas pageant while I was growing up was a triptych of birth stories concerning Jesus, Buddha, and Confucius, with its clear message that beneath the colorful and engaging differences of cultural detail lay a common moral about the specialness and immense potential of every newborn child, anywhere. What was sacred was not Baby Jesus—nor, of course, Baby Buddha or Baby Confucius either—but the mystery of birth; each night a child is born is a holy night, indeed.

The cultural construct of Christmas offered two other paradigmatic images. One was the figure of Santa Claus, presented from my earliest memory as an amusing fairy tale, literal belief in which was reserved for those less intellectually competent; an exact and overt analog to the conventional notion of God. The other was a seasonal softening of the stark aesthetic of modernist intellectualism, with its eschewal of ornamentation. We Humanists might not believe anything much about Christmas, but for the month of December it was acceptable to enjoy a sparkling, fanciful, gilded, bedecked, abundant Victorian sensibility that we would hold to be beneath us throughout the rest of the year.

All these assorted influences left me with an enduring rational rejection of an anthropomorphic Father God in the sky, and an equally inescapable hunger for a vocabulary to describe, express, summon, and share the experience of primal reverence that is utterly real and precious in my life. I discovered neo-Paganism as a theological student and very young minister when it arose in the UU movement in the late 1970s and early 80s. It connected with my aesthetic, liturgical, and spiritual hunger in several ways.

First, as a second-wave feminist seeking institutional authority for religious leadership, the exploration of feminine images of the divine was engaging to me. My upbringing had more or less forbidden me the concept of a monotheistic masculine god; however, it had said nothing about not believing in the Goddess, or goddesses! I understood diversity in my spiritual bones; Paganism offered a variety of soft and playful mythologies that did not depend upon intellectual assent for effectiveness. It celebrated female creativity and strength, and acknowledged the paradoxical destructiveness that is inherent in the natural world and the human condition. With Paganism, the long-ago permission for wonder at the robin's corpse and the bean sprout, and the resonance of the scenic duck pond in the cemetery, became grounded in a tradition of sorts, and the species egotism of Humanism found relief in the idea of a religion that could be Earth-centered.

Paganism also helped to resolve my liturgical dilemma. The Unitarian Universalism of my childhood was thin on ceremony, and my occasional attempts to fit my longing for worship into the structures of traditional Christianity ended up feeling like cultural misappropriation in its most disingenuous form. My guide to Pagan ritual, quoting I know not whom, once told me, "We practice our religion exactly the way our ancestors did millennia ago; we make it up!" With this permission in hand, I have come to understand that my style of preference is in fact deeply informed by Puritan/modernist simplicity, the theological approach of the via negativa, which examines what God is *not*, and rationalism. There is a strand in Pagan ritual that often strikes me as willfully silly, inviting me beyond my capacity to suspend disbelief. I'm just not ecstatic enough for spiral dances. Nevertheless, it has been helpful to understand that specific theologies do not own candles or flowers or scented smoke or postures or gestures or wine or water or bread or any other archetypal human experience or image. And pretty shiny things can be evocative all year round.

As I begin my seventh decade as a practicing Unitarian Universalist, my theological tent remains firmly pitched in the soil of Humanism. Yet I am entirely without patience for the perpetual debate about who is now allegedly being excluded from the ranks of our theology or ministry or con-gregations. Among the traditional theists, the Humanists, and the Pagans, each has common cause with the others against the third, and it's time that we grow up enough to recognize these affinities. The Humanists and the Pagans rightfully regard with misgiving the cultural hegemony and assumption of privilege of theists—especially Christians —particularly on behalf of monotheism and the patri-arch of the Hebrew and Christian scriptures. There are more things in heaven and Earth than are dreamed of in this philosophy—a lot more. The Pagans and the theists together take rightful exception to the dry prose and self-idolatry of Humanism, which has yet to demonstrate the epistemological modesty appropriate to beings who do not have complete access to our own motivations. Reason unsupported by enacted narrative and community attach-ment will always be vulnerable to dangerous superstition and mobs. Finally, the Humanists and the theists are correct to insist on the transformative vector of history and mental rigor, viewing with justified suspicion unsupported claims of an idealized past or the simplistic goodness of nature. There is a tragic dignity to human self-awareness that is honored by the emotional self-restraint of intellectual effort, and a sense of the ridiculous is not exclusively a function of repression.

Both Paganism and Humanism have served historically to move Unitarian Universalism into a novel religious realm, transcending its roots in Christianity and creating a new understanding of spiritual community. In no way do I want to see our Christian heritage eliminated, or those who find it their most congenial path excluded; at the same time, neither am I willing to be confined by it.

⊷⊶

KENDYL L. R. GIBBONS *is minister at All Souls Unitarian Universalist Church in Kansas City. Prior to that, she served congregations in Naperville, Illinois, and Minneapolis. She is a lifelong Unitarian Universalist and past president of the Unitarian Universalist Ministers Association. She is also an adjunct faculty member at Meadville Lombard Theological School in Chicago.*

Affirming LGBTQ Identity in UU Paganism

Michael Walker

O, Spirit of Life, we call out to You!

We, Children of the Earth of all different kinds, call to You,
The inseparable Mother Earth and Father Sky,
God-Goddess of Life and Love, the Source of Souls.

Shoulder to shoulder, in the light of the moon, we stand.
In a circle inscribed by our will, cast between the worlds,
In a time that is beyond all time, we stand, together.

Baring our naked souls before all that is Holy,
We cast off petty differences, we let them fall away,
Finding ourselves each unique and beloved as we are.

Mother-Father God, O Holy One of Many Names,
We are gathered, so many lost and imperfect souls!

And yet, having found each other, we have also found You.

May it ever be so and blessed be you all.

Circles of people gather in the chapels or courtyards of many Unitarian Universalist churches each month on the full moon, often speaking words something like the invocation above. They gather to honor the cycles of nature, the forces of life and love in the world, and the best selves of each person present. At one such moon gathering, I recall a friend of mine—a big, balding man dressed in a beautiful satin gown—serving as the priestess for the ritual, invoking a queer aspect of the God/dess. A common Pagan understanding of the various names of old gods and goddesses is that they are all aspects or archetypes of the One. With a twinkle in his eye and a huge grin, my friend and others led a beautiful ritual that affirmed each person present, whatever their sexual orientation or gender identity. This is not a fluke; such open and affirming rites have been occurring at UU congregations for decades.

A confluence of events has brought us to this place of acceptance, although the road has never been easy. Beginning with the 1970 General Assembly, the Unitarian Universalist Association has repeatedly affirmed our collective support of lesbian, gay, bisexual, transgender, and queer (LGBTQ) communities. For at least that long, various Pagan communities and traditions have likewise voiced similar support and acceptance, which went hand-in-hand with a burgeoning feminist-spirituality movement. Raising consciousness about an ethic of equity and equality for feminism in religion resulted in the gathering of numerous circles of women, womyn, and sometimes allied men. In an effort to raise consciousness, some educators designed curricula that taught women-centered or women-honoring folklore and mythos. Two such curricula include *Cakes for the Queen of Heaven* by Shirley Ann Ranck (1986) and *Rise Up & Call Her Name* by Elizabeth Fisher (1995). These curricula continue to be used to offer feminist spirituality and women-affirming courses in UU congregations. A happy side effect of raising feminist consciousness is that it has paved the way for raising consciousness about other identities, including LGBTQ-specific identities.

Two other historical events have influenced how UU congregations have responded to Pagans in their midst. The organizers of what became the Covenant of Unitarian Universalist Pagans (CUUPS) gathered at the UUA General Assembly in 1985. Precisely ten years later, after lobbying by CUUPS and many other Earth-focused Unitarian Universalists, the General Assembly adopted the sixth Source of Unitarian Universalism: "Spiritual teachings of Earth-centered traditions which celebrate the sacred circle of life and instruct us to live in harmony with the rhythms of nature." With resolutions recognizing the contributions of feminist, LGBT, and now Pagan-identified people, the door was opened wide, welcoming in those who may have been on the margins before. This has long been a hallmark of Unitarian Universalism—while other denominations circle the wagons and find ways to shut out people from the margins, we've been inviting people from the margins to come into the sanctuary and be part of our community. Those of us whose identities intersect or overlap find a welcoming word and smile when we walk through the sanctuary doors. It cannot be overstated that finding or creating safe space is important for all people, and is especially important for LGBTQ people who find little of it in other places in their lives. The openness of Unitarian Universalism to Paganism has provided safe havens for seekers of all kinds. Over the years, I have particularly noted the importance of this openness for youth.

During a period of service at Rowe Camp and Conference Center in Western Massachusetts, which has Unitarian Universalist connections, I received a call from a colleague in the UU ministry. She was concerned about a young member of her congregation, a teenager who identified as a transgender male and Pagan. This person had experienced harassment, shunning, and emotional pain at school, to the point that his mother pulled him from school and began homeschooling. I cannot convey the full story of this young person's life, except to say that being accepted and welcomed was a foreign experience to him. My colleague had hoped that the summer camp at Rowe would be a sanctuary and welcoming community for her young parishioner. Indeed, like UU congregations across the country, UU camps (including Rowe) have long been open and affirming communities of caring people from all walks of life. I was delighted to observe, over the term of summer camp, that this young man found community. His whole self, including his Unitarian Universalist, Pagan, and transgender aspects, were accepted as small parts of who he was. When the camp was over, he told me that he was thrilled to get to know this community and feel part of it. His delight was apparent, and a far cry from the dejected state he was in when he arrived there earlier in the summer.

I believe many factors have allowed us to create such a safe and welcoming space as this young man found. Unitarian Universalists have often, year after year, found new doors to open, new social justice causes to embrace, new people from the margins to invite in. We have embraced feminist spirituality, LGBTQ rights, Earth-based spirituality, and many other facets of life and society, all of which inspired Unitarian Universalists to stretch themselves and make room at the table for more people, including those who may be different from themselves.

Another factor has been our attention to how we use language in ritual and theology. Just as previous generations worked for feminist ideals and gender-neutral religious language, younger generations have made room for the queering of theology. It seems to me that both of these changes are a logical evolution of the Universalist strand of UU history. Universal salvation—salvation for all, rather than predestination—led our forebears to posit a loving God who damns no one to hell. Feminist thought advocated that we expand the concept of God to God-Goddess (or

God/dess), Mother-Father God, or other formulations, such as Spirit of Life. Feminist spirituality raised our consciousness, clearing the path for many new ways of being, not the least of which has been making room for women—and later LGBTQ-identified people—in religious leadership, as well as gender-neutral or inclusive language in worship services and hymnody, and providing safe space for members of the LGBTQ community. Now, the queering of theology allows us to envision God as either multi-gendered or ungendered, or both, knowing that the mystery that is God (using a name we humans know), is truly unknowable and indescribable. Queer theology posits that we have always had LGBTQ people throughout history. And, if this is true, what does this say about our relationship to the holy? The influence of queer theology allows us to say, "You know, we Westerners like to say that we are created in His image. What if it's really that we are created is *His-Her-Their* image, an image that is multitudinous and diverse, allowing each of us, no matter who we are, to share in the glory of God?" That formulation is a queering of theology from a Christian perspective, obviously, but may be most recognizable to the reader.

If we are to attempt the queering of theology from a Pagan perspective, we can call upon queer aspects of the holy, naming the divine in all its diverse manifestations, making room for a diversity of humanity too. Mythology is replete with stories of gay and lesbian gods/goddesses and genderless, multi-gendered, or intersex god/desses. Straight and bisexual, too. Dig into mythology long enough, and one can find enough stories to match the wide tapestry of human experience. There is something that any person can resonate with, and that is important. Unitarian Universalists, Pagans, and UU Pagans do not subscribe to a static theological catechism or standardized doctrine. We find inspiration in many sources, and what is better than to find inspiration in a source that helps us find meaning and joy in our own lives? Knowing this, any one of us can become a priest/ess of the God/dess, in any of the many forms.

‹o›

MICHAEL WALKER *is a Unitarian Universalist minister, who came to this ministry after serving for more than twenty years as a Pagan priest. He served on the board of CUUPS for six years, including two years as vice president. He is working on a long-term goal of establishing a spiritual retreat, children's summer camp, and nature preserve in the Pacific Northwest* (www.uucascadesretreat.org).

A WICCAN ALLY'S PERSPECTIVE

MICHELLE MUELLER

I decided I was Wiccan when I first read *Wicca: A Guide for the Solitary Practitioner* by Scott Cunningham. This was in 1996, and I was twelve and a half. Since then, I have met many others who were introduced to the Craft through Scott Cunningham's books. We could call this my conversion text, although many Witches and Pagans prefer the phrase "coming home." I practiced as a solitary for seven years and joined an eclectic coven as a sophomore in college. In 2005, after I moved to California to attend seminary, I joined a Gardnerian group, Coven Trismegiston, in Berkeley. Gardnerian Craft, along with the Alexandrian tradition (into which prolific authors Janet and Stewart Farrar were initiated), is known as a form of British Traditional Wicca, ceremonial traditions of Wicca from the United Kingdom. We meet at the covenstead for full moons and have open Sabbats at the equinoxes, solstices and cross-quarter days (Samhain, Imbolc, Beltaine, and Lammas—the rough midpoints between each equinox and solstice).

Like many others who discovered Wicca and Paganism in their youth, I was engulfed by reverence for the Earth, mythologies of the Goddess, and psychic and occult arts. Members of my generation turned to Paganism and UU Paganism largely on account of ecology. We learned about environmentalism in school. We learned about climate change, which we called global warming until recently. We may not have all known the full science behind climate change, but public-school teachers in my time knew that actions for the environment were indeed important. Concern for the environment, while not always put into practice, was a theoretical given in my public education.

I practiced as a solitary Wiccan in my youth, performing full-moon rituals in the backyard late nights and honoring the Sabbats on my own or with an occasional close friend who was interested, supportive, or just curious. I joined an adult coven in Philadelphia during my sophomore year of college. I observed many residential Wiccan and Pagan students remain on-campus with their religious practice. I sought intergenerational Pagan mentorship and practiced with a group outside of the college, in addition to helping to form a student group at my college. When I moved to Berkeley for my master's degree program, I joined the Gardnerian coven I currently participate in. The priestess and priest of the coven officiated the handfasting (a Pagan commitment ceremony) between my partner and me in June 2015.

I began as a director of religious education right out of seminary. I found a posting on Craigslist for a three-quarter-time position as acting director of religious education at the Unitarian Universalist Church in Cherry Hill, New Jersey. I expressed in my application that I had been looking for *just such a position.* At my parents' house, I lived less than five miles from the parish.

I had known of this Unitarian Universalist congregation since youth and had attended one or two events there. I was not raised Unitarian Universalist. (Neither was I raised Wiccan.) But, as a Wiccan youth and young adult, I recognized Unitarian Universalists as allies, on account of their multireligious inclusion, emphasis on social justice, and care for the Earth (the seventh Principle). I applied immediately and was hired within a week or so.

I worked as acting director of religious education for this congregation for two and a half years, until I felt ready to return to graduate school for my PhD. For two and a half years I did not identify as Unitarian Universalist. "I am Wiccan. I consider myself an ally to Unitarian Universalists," I said to countless families, as the director of religious education of the UU church.

No one was concerned, although I got used to people forgetting my identity and introducing me to others as a Unitarian Universalist or UU Pagan anyway. I realized the distinction was far more important to me than it was to the families of our church.

As I started my doctoral program in 2011, I also began a part-time director of religious education position at the First Unitarian Universalist Church of Stockton in the Central Valley of California, fifty miles from Berkeley. Parents and congregation members there reacted pretty much the same to my Wiccan identity as they had in suburban New Jersey. It was far more important to *me* to keep up the boundary, and generally people would forget and call me a Unitarian Universalist anyway.

By the end of my time there, I had found that I may as well be saying, "I could be a Unitarian Universalist." Over time, that was how I felt. I have identified as a Wiccan because I discovered it at the right time. As a very loyal person, I believe I would have been a Unitarian Universalist for life had I been raised in that tradition, a liberal religion similar to my own Wiccan faith.

Here are some reasons why I could be a Unitarian Universalist. I will comment on my relationship with each of the seven Principles on which Unitarian Universalist Association congregations agree. These are Principles that member congregations "affirm and promote," according to the UUA bylaws. In children's religious education, we teach the Principles in age-appropriate children's language. Due to my background in religious education, I reference both versions of the Principles.

The first Principle: *The inherent worth and dignity of every person*. As a Wiccan, I refer to the *sacredness and divinity of every individual*, which is, practically speaking, equivalent.

We should recognize each person's dignity—or divinity if you prefer—and approach them recognizing this. We may not always agree with them, but we should respect the divine being that they are.

The second Principle: *Justice, equity, and compassion in human relations*. As a Pagan, I broaden this statement to include relations with animals and plants, for that is the Pagan contribution, and often an issue raised by UU Pagans.

The third Principle: *Acceptance of one another and encouragement to spiritual growth in our congregations*. Like Unitarian Universalists, I—as a Pagan—support spiritual growth for all.

The fourth Principle: *A free and responsible search for truth and meaning*. Witches and Pagans have strong senses of searching for what is true. Generally, worldwide contemporary Pagans and Wiccans believe that there is more than one way to truth. Wicca, for those who follow it, is one spiritual path among many that helps people understand the meaning and spirituality of life and the connectedness of all things. We therefore keep sacred our own search for what is true, and support others in their search for what is true. As a religious educator, I know that Unitarian Universalist religious education supports children and youth as they explore their own search for what is true. We find an example in the credo-writing process, a component of most UU Coming of Age programs.

The fifth Principle: *The right of conscience and the use of the democratic process within our congregations and in society at large*. In children's religious education, we express the Principle this way: "We believe that all persons should have a vote about the things that concern them." Within and outside of our congregations, people should have a say in issues that affect them. There is not one decision-making process accepted by all Wiccan or Pagan groups. However, most employ some use of the democratic process, factoring individual members' votes into decisions that affect them, and most Pagans support a democratic process for society. I participate in an organization called the Covenant of the Goddess. We have a meeting similar to the Unitarian Universalist Association's General Assembly. Our Grand Council is held annually by a different Local Council every summer. We hold elections for national-board officers democratically. We actually require consensus of all member covens and member solitary caucuses in order to take an action, such as amending bylaws, at Grand Council.

The sixth Principle: *The goal of world community with peace, liberty, and justice for all*. Recently I attended the Parliament of the World's Religions, an organization "created to cultivate harmony among the world's religious and spiritual communities and foster their engagement with the world." I have attended this event in Spain and Australia over the last decade with Wiccans, Pagans, Unitarian Universalists, and representatives from other world faiths around me. I have taught my humanities students at Berkeley City College about important social movements including Black Lives Matter and womanist, mujerista, feminist, and

LGBTQQIAA movements. Advocating for social justice is an important aspect of the sixth Principle.

Most contemporary Pagan practitioners do not see their traditions as the only pathways toward spiritual fulfillment. Today's Pagans generally embrace the ideal of pluralism, a mindset I believe a peaceful world community requires. If we cannot accept the validity of beliefs other than our own, we can never live harmoniously alongside other peoples. Pluralism means standing with Pagan cultures and non-Pagans across time and space around the world, accepting diversity as a positive.

The seventh Principle: *Respect for the interdependent web of all existence of which we are a part.* This is of utmost importance to Wiccans, Pagans, and UU Pagans and has further drawn those of Pagan leanings into the Unitarian Universalist Association. It is also likely an influential factor for the development of the Covenant of Unitarian Universalist Pagans (CUUPS), the UUA affinity group that merges Unitarian Universalism and Paganism. For children, we express the seventh Principle as "We believe in caring for our planet Earth, the home we share with all living things." Both versions—"the interdependent web" and "home for all living things"—resonate so powerfully with my Pagan perspective that I prefer not to choose between them.

These are Principles that I can agree with, that I can get behind. I've known this from the beginning. Until recently, I've been an ally to Unitarian Universalism. After five years of close work in UU organizations, close personal relationships with UU adults, and nurturing the religious and spiritual development of children and youth in Unitarian Universalism, I am no longer just an ally. *I could be a Unitarian Universalist.* My Pagan identity continues to be dominant. But when it comes down to it, *I could be a Unitarian Universalist.*

—◦—

MICHELLE MUELLER *describes herself as a Pagan "who could be a UU"—a phrase she developed in a guest sermon on faith formation for the Live Oak UU Fellowship in Alameda, California, after serving as their director of religious education (DRE) for a year. She is a Wiccan and member of the Covenant of the Goddess. She has served as a DRE for congregations in New Jersey and California.*

Welcoming the Gods
into Our Congregation

Sue Nading

Whatever religions you have known, whatever god you accept or deny, whatever your heritage or culture: you are welcome here. Whoever you are, whomever you love, whatever body you live in: you are welcome here.
—Unitarian Universalist Association website

This concept of welcoming different spiritualities or beliefs is a cornerstone of Unitarian Universalism, a rich and diverse religion that encourages people to seek their own path, whether Christian, Humanist, Buddhist, Pagan, or Earth-centered, or one of many others represented around the world. All are welcome here.

Unitarian Universalism offers the opportunity not only to encourage but also to celebrate different religious heritages and customs. Our spiritual beliefs need to ground and support us but not restrict us in our interactions with other faiths. It is this challenge to look beyond our differences and even our similarities that we need to meet in order to create strong unified communities of diverse perspectives and insights. We all run the risk of holding too tightly to our particular spiritualities without gracefully and respectfully allowing others the space to explore and deepen their own.

As explicit as Unitarian Universalist proclamations of openness and respect toward diverse beliefs may be, Pagan and Earth-centered people can face particular challenges as the congregation attempts to act it out in daily life. But a covenanted community that takes this welcome seriously and personally can commit to it. Such a community can work through the challenges and end up stronger for having widened its embrace.

For example, some at Peoples Unitarian Universalist Church in Cedar Rapids, where I am a member, viewed Pagans cautiously, even suspiciously. Perhaps it was because of how we dressed or even how we freely embraced our spirituality—both were so different and stood out in the community. It is part of the nature of our Pagan practice to hold ceremonies, classes, and events outside of the normal worship schedule, and we freely invite one and all to attend. Some members of the congregation questioned our heavy use of the church's space given that they felt we did not contribute enough financially to the church overall. They felt that we were disproportionately availing ourselves of the church's resources without truly giving back. However,

Pagans have had a strong tradition of volunteering within our church in the religious education program (both children and adult), social justice activities, and even worship committees.

This situation was a symptom of the larger culture that implicitly values financial pledges more than volunteering and being a good community steward. There may have been some other unexamined cultural assumptions about Pagans as well, coupled with personal biases, fears, or misconceptions. At first, the tensions were exacerbated by questions that reflected common misunderstandings: Were Pagans also being respectful of other beliefs? Were they truly welcoming those of other beliefs to attend events? Did they really need to meet and celebrate that much?

This all came to a head when the congregation became divided over whether to sell our church building after many years of debate. Many Pagans within our community were adamantly opposed to selling the building because of personal memories and its rich history; including its use by members of the American Indian Movement during a 1975 federal-court trial related to their occupation of the town of Wounded Knee. A vote to sell the building failed at least three times before it finally passed, much to the anguish and disappointment of members of the Pagan community.

During this time many Pagans retreated back into their own insular group and isolated themselves from the rest of the congregation, becoming defensive and emotional toward those who did not share their pain and sense of outrage. Old misconceptions and resentments flared into new arguments and discord, which threatened to kill our fledgling sense of unified purpose and community. We were losing track of our identity, our community, and even our beliefs as a result of the discord following our welcoming of others and their gods. It was an environment of distrust, lack of understanding, and miscommunication.

We could have abandoned our mission as it appeared to have abandoned us, but as Unitarian Universalist minister Nancy Shaffer noted, there comes a point when that is not an option and we must take a higher path. In her book *When There Is Still Light*, she writes, "It isn't love that makes the world go round but compassion—starting over in gentleness when love hasn't been enough or other factors have failed: a gentle refusal to blame oneself or others and just begin again."

Through the efforts of our leaders and members, Peoples Church continues to work through the aftermath of these events. It has not been easy. Some people left. But others stayed and worked at it, sometimes worked at it without hope or knowing that it would all work out. Our Pagan group leaders encouraged discussion and learning, both within the group and with other members of the congregation. And, in fact, the group grew during this time.

As it turned out, the Pagan community grew to more than three times its original size in the new building. I believe that this growth and resilience has created a new impression of Pagans for the congregation. We are no longer the outsiders but an integral part of the congregation. Tensions do still arise because of the fear of what is different, but I think we have grown as a congregation, and I hope we will continue to do so, welcoming all to share all the gifts of their personal spiritualities.

Members of our congregation's Pagan community have held and currently hold prominent roles not only in the religious-education program and worship and welcoming committees, but also on the board of trustees. For example, our Pagan community has worked side by side with others within the congregation to host annual fall celebrations, most specifically those activities around Halloween. As new members and staff join our congregation, issues have surfaced about who will lead and organize different activities and even whether certain activities should be part of the celebration.

It would be easy to allow our differences of faith and custom to drive us apart. Any compromise means that someone has to give up something familiar and comfortable. But all of our spiritual leaders at Peoples Church realize that our strength as a congregation lies in our ability to work together and create a richer experience for everyone. It has made our Halloween and Samhain celebrations very memorable and inclusive, and I believe everyone now finds them richer and more satisfying as a result of the collaboration.

We have learned that differences don't keep us from working together, only resistance to finding common ground. Recently, our congregation faced a tremendous

upheaval when our minister moved on to another congregation, which brought a number of conflicts within the
congregation out into the open. The continued viability of
the congregation was in serious question. Several members
of the congregation organized a number of talking circles
to work through the issues in very productive and moving ways. All members were invited, and the diversity of
viewpoints and beliefs in these respectful talking circles
has allowed for the process of healing and fellowship to
continue to this day. It was important that *all* members,
including Pagans, were considered vital to the effort
because we needed to understand who we truly were as
a congregation. If Pagans were still regarded as outsiders,
merely guests using the building when this tumultuous
time began, the congregation might never have been able
to come together and heal itself. This was one of the best
examples of the fruits of religious belief as described by
retired UU minister Alice Blair Wesley: "Whatever our theological persuasion, Unitarian Universalists generally agree
that the fruits of religious belief matter more than beliefs
about religion—even about God. So we usually speak more
of the fruits: gratitude for blessings, worthy aspirations, the
renewal of hope, and service on behalf of justice."

All members, Pagan and non-Pagan, are benefitting
from the unification of our community. It has allowed us
to mount successful fundraising campaigns, social events,
and community-building opportunities. When our Pagan
group hosts events, we have always welcomed all members

of the congregation to participate. Now, however, these are no longer seen as specifically Pagan events, but rather church community events, in a general sense.

These special events and community gatherings provide the most visible result of our hard work to build bridges, but it is our congregation's weekly worship service that stabilizes these efforts and provides a solid foundation for our community. Our services are thought provoking and inclusive, incorporating rituals and ceremonies from Earth-centered traditions as well as from Christian, Jewish, Buddhist, and many other traditions. We have worshipped side by side and grown in the knowledge and experience of a vast array of the world's spiritual wisdom. Many members of our community now look forward to seasonal Pagan celebrations like Yule, which highlight our ability to welcome different spiritualities and their traditions for the benefit of everyone.

Of course, these services would not be meaningful or unifying without the efforts of those in our religious education programs. We have a strong history of supporting not only the youth in our church but the adults as well. Recently we hired a new director of religious education and found that the existing curriculum needed to be revamped and made more inclusive. She did not have any knowledge or experience regarding Pagan beliefs and practices but energetically embraced the challenge of broadening the program to include Pagan-related material and making it even more successful. This would not be possible without the willingness of the congregation to support and engage all faiths. Pagans within the church leadership saw this as an opportunity not only to educate but also to strengthen existing relationships and perhaps address misconceptions Pagans and non-Pagans unconsciously held about each other. Many of our Pagan community stepped forward to organize and help teach within the program.

However, as with most journeys, there are many opportunities to trip and fall or lose our way. These pitfalls have caused us to hesitate and even second-guess ourselves. But our seven Principles, particularly the one affirming "acceptance of one another and encouragement to spiritual growth in our congregations," have allowed us to successfully maneuver through weariness and conflicts. Changes in ministry, administrative staff, and even congregational membership have caused concern and tension, causing some of us to question each other's motives, at times. But we are learning to embrace change, to welcome it as it furthers rather than impedes our growth.

As a group, we eventually found our footing and emerged as stronger members of Peoples Church. Conflicts within our group and the church at large caused us to bravely face our own shortcomings and embrace our strengths. We intentionally became more involved and affirmed a common bond—that we are all Unitarian Universalists. Our congregation developed a new covenant of right relations to help guide us in our interactions, and we have continued to build new circles of relationship within our Pagan group, with our congregation, and with our community at large.

New challenges continue to present themselves, but we move forward with a new understanding that exclusion and fear of difference deprive us of the very energy and vitality that we need to overcome challenges and to thrive as a beloved community of people who follow a variety of spiritual paths.

—◦—

SUE NADING *is a freelance writer who lives in Cedar Rapids, Iowa, with her husband and four children. She is a past board member of Peoples Unitarian Universalist Church in Cedar Rapids and has been a member of her local chapter of CUUPS since 2008.*

A Journey of Service

Jerrie Kishpaugh Hildebrand

Service has always defined my spirituality, faith, and heart. As a Unitarian Universalist Pagan, it is one of the things that drew me to both paths almost at the same time. I have always thought that religion or spiritual practices unexpressed in the world through action and service felt empty. This commitment to service is what I loved about my youth group and my religious community growing up as a Presbyterian in a small rural town. Service fills my heart and allows me to know I make a difference in the world, however small.

My journey into Paganism and Unitarian Universalism came after years of searching for a place where I could fully express myself. I did not want to deny my past in Christianity. I wanted to express my heart, tied to honoring the Earth as my home, and to Spirit. I wanted to be known as the woman I am, who holds the Earth as sacred, and stands with people who bring different points of view to the table. I did not want to be defined by labels, nor to label anyone else.

I often think of the days when I would sit along the Susquehanna River in my youth. Watching the river flow by while I was tucked under the lilac trees and lilies of the valley growing wild. Warm spring and summer days after a gentle rain brought out all of the smells around me. The freshly planted dirt of the garden abounded in the farm fields. This was where the holy lived for me. The plants and animals were interdependent, almost appearing in a dance with one another, feeding and serving one another. I was reminded of the stories of gods and goddesses of ancient cities I read about when I was a girl.

The small rural community I lived in overflowed with opportunities to be of service. My father was a volunteer fireman, my mother volunteered with the firemen's auxiliary. Both were part of other civic and fraternal service organizations in town. My sisters and I volunteered not only at the fire department but also with our youth groups at the local Presbyterian church and 4-H. I belonged to Constellations, a Masonic order for young women. I loved the kind of service that impacted a community and broke down walls that kept people from understanding and caring for each other. My visions and thoughts of this kind of service often felt like a tall order for one person or a small group of people. I have learned all too intimately, however, that service can become the norm if we choose to embrace the idea.

In Paganism, I often was left feeling like no one really cared about this kind of service. Sure, people volunteered for their group's gatherings, festivals, and daily work to grow and keep the organizations going, but nothing bigger. My desire was the opposite, even though I understood the concerns of others who wanted to focus on working for only our own groups. It felt insular and isolating. If we were working more outside of our groups in food pantries, in homeless shelters, or in interfaith settings, our communities would learn that Pagans were like any other faith community. Nothing weird about us at all, we just saw some things differently. I was always left wondering how to affect the discourses about thinking differently and participating with the communities I lived in.

A young woman in the Girl Scout troop I was leading invited me to come to her UU church. Her family explained what Unitarian Universalism was and how welcome I would be. What they told me was familiar to me, with conversations about various service projects they were involved in. I saw a possibility in what they were up to, but how could I fit in as a Pagan in a UU setting? In a church? My first step was being up front about my path and beliefs. I became the first "out" Pagan to join the congregation.

Each week in our worship service, we spoke the affirmation of faith. I felt something tug at me:

> Love is the spirit of this church,
> the quest for truth is its sacrament
> and service is its prayer.

This is our covenant; to dwell together in peace,
to seek knowledge in freedom,
and to help those in need.

Thus do we covenant with each other
and with God (Goddess).

I felt freed up saying it. Around me sat many people of other spiritual orientations. Christians, Jews, Humanists, atheists, Pagans, and others, all speaking the same declaration in unison, standing as one denomination. They even included the Goddess in the language. There was something about it that was exhilarating and gave me an odd sense of peace. It was like I could just be. Be myself.

I continued my affiliation with Pagan organizations, and stood with groups that did not require dogmatic approaches to service and did not expect me to follow a certain set of beliefs. Interestingly, I was looked at as a UU Pagan within these groups. UU Paganism and Earth/nature-centered spirituality was a growing group within the denomination. I just continued being myself but in the reverse, as a Pagan UU! I stepped up and created at our congregation a chapter of the Covenant of Unitarian Universalist Pagans, the continental Pagan organization within the UUA. This became a gathering place for UU Pagans, Pagan UUs, and many others in the community who honored Earth/nature-centered traditions and wanted someplace welcoming to gather. Soon I found myself on the continental board of trustees of and supporting other Pagan-related causes.

At the same time, I discovered the work of Lady Liberty League (LLL), a religious-freedom organization standing for the civil rights of people in Earth/nature-centered faiths and spiritual paths, which seemed like a natural fit for me. Religious freedom issues arise in every area of life. Lady Liberty League steps up to support Pagans from many traditions, and has collaborated with Unitarian Universalists for a long time. They have tackled custody cases, school systems, prisons, employment settings, and more. The LLL team networks and finds what is needed to support someone. Little did I realize that through my work with LLL I would be engaging with the national political scene. I thought of myself as an artist, not an activist, although time would show otherwise.

In 1999, Senator Bob Barr did not like that the US military had approved the right for Wiccans, Pagans, and practitioners of Earth/nature-centered faiths to have worship services at military installations. He worked to amend a defense-authorization bill in order to prohibit the practice of these religions at Defense Department facilities. LLL organizers got into action. We networked with senators and representatives of our own states, and got the word out to our communities. Senator Barr's measure was defeated.

The day I heard this news, it became clear to me that a small group of people could do anything. I also became aware of how religious freedom is never guaranteed and we always need to be vigilant about our civil liberties. Despite never believing I would I have been standing for something this strongly, I started working more with LLL and Circle Sanctuary, a nature-centered church and nature preserve, on these kinds of projects.

Back home in Salem, Massachusetts, I found myself sitting at the table with community and faith leaders addressing issues of hate and how to work together. We developed the No Place for Hate Committee with the mayor and others. It was good to be part of this, as some of the people in the group understood what it was to stand for something bigger. No matter what group I worked with, I was always public about being Unitarian Universalist and Pagan. I did not apologize for one moment, and I was totally welcomed. Soon, other Wiccan and Pagan leaders joined the group, lending their voices and working to make Salem live up to its designation as the "City of Peace." Over time, even local tourism groups began to learn how to speak about the word *Witch* in ways that did not just refer to the people murdered and accused as such in the seventeenth century. The groups began to educate tourists who come to Salem. I can see this change continuing even now. Today we are a city that challenges hate, bigotry, and discrimination. In many ways, I see where that small group that gathered years ago has made a difference in how Wiccans, Witches, and Pagans are treated here today.

So, what else would the gods and goddesses bring that a small group could have an impact on? At times I really needed to consider a break. Between my responsibilities as board co-chair at my church, serving on the CUUPS board of trustees, working with LLL, running my business, being a mom to an incredible young boy, as well as being a wife, breaks and rest were rare. Some of the ministers around me, though, would joke that I was ignoring the calling that was knocking at my door. I figured I might have been, but I also knew I could not fully hear what was knocking. I kept thinking, "Pagans don't have ministers." But I would come to understand, over time, that priests and priestesses in Pagan traditions and traditions of the Earth are ministers and caretakers just like traditional ones!

At this same time another issue with Pagans and Wiccans in the military reared its head. Pagan men and women, who had earned the right to have government-issued headstones, were unable to have their markers inscribed with their religious symbol, the pentacle. From 1997 to 2007, groups had worked to change this. As the Iraq War continued, Pagan soldiers were dying and requests for headstones with pentacles were being denied. Discussions with the Department of Veterans Affairs ended in stalemates. Pagan churches and organizations applied on behalf of families and were also given excuses. One evening I received a call from the LLL team asking if I would be willing to jump into supporting them in this quest. Being a former Navy wife, this made me so mad that I wholeheartedly agreed!

Widows of current soldiers who had died were ready to go. The organization Americans United for the Separation of Church and State had taken on the case. Hundreds of Earth/nature-centered organizations pulled together to work with LLL, as did other faith communities. Pagan churches that had reached out in the past to support families found a renewed commitment to getting this handled. Paperwork and files over the years had been shelved. Correspondence between the Veterans Administration and other government agencies was released, and the discrimination came to light.

This all angered me so much! I wondered why. I was not in the military. It did not affect me. It was not my life. It was, however, an issue of equality, fairness, and honor of the lives of those who served our country. My relatives were all retired or currently serving military. I would be furious if I could not honor their faith designations on their memorial markers. Again, ministers, priests, and priestesses nudged me about this calling they sensed, but I continued to deflect the notion of that kind of service.

Then came nights of being on the phone into the wee hours. From Salem to Wisconsin to California to Texas to the South, Pagan leaders from many traditions were organizing, talking, and lobbying. I became the voice of UU Pagans in this effort. I used to get off the phone at times feeling so fed up with my country that I wanted to move. But every time I heard that other faith communities were backing us, my faith was renewed. It is one thing to have one's own community calling senators, representatives, and government connections, but it is an entirely different thing when people of other faith communities wrap their arms around the idea that freedom of religion means all religions. Whenever I talked with a Unitarian Universalist about the situation, I knew that a call or letter would go out and would add to the voices of many. Even *UU World* reported on the situation with an incredible article encouraging Unitarian Universalists to support the cause.

I was asked to start illustrating designs of the pentacle so some consensus could be created on which style to use. In the evenings, I would go into my studio, light a simple candle and a stick of incense. I would quietly reflect on the intention of the illustration and those who had served our country. Later, leaders from many Pagan organizations talked and discerned the best version to send to the VA and the Pentagon. On April 23, 2007, at about 4:30am, I received a call to send my illustration of the pentacle to a list of government agencies. As I crawled back into bed for a few last minutes of sleep, I realized what had just happened. By the time most people woke the next day, the pentacle was to be added as the 37th symbol for military headstones, opening the door for many other symbols of faith in the Earth/nature-centered communities that had faced similar discrimination to be added as well.

During that time, I could see that Unitarian Universalists were not the only ones who could stand in the affirmation of faith. Pagans could hold L. Griswold Williams's covenant of love as the spirit, with the quest for truth as their sacrament, and service as their prayer, along with practitioners of many other religions. I also saw how people of all religions could stand in support of one another.

Today, UU Pagans serve in many places in the Unitarian Universalist and Pagan communities, making a difference locally, regionally, and nationally, with some working internationally in settings such as the Parliament of the World's Religions. We have made and will continue to make a difference, no longer needing to buy into the notion that oppression is inevitable. There is dignity in unapologetically being oneself. This idea fosters understanding so much more than trying to fit in.

So what was that calling others saw that I did not? Ministry! Not in the context of being a UU minister, but in ministering to and with the larger Pagan community. I never knew that the word *reverend* or *minister* could be associated with Paganism. I knew that I was respected and making a difference. Then I looked up the meanings and the etymology of the words. Reverend means "worthy of respect" and minister means "to render service or aid." Everything started to make sense. I laughed as I began to understand why others viewed me in this light! I saw that I was resisting putting a name to what I was already doing. After many years in service to my faith communities, in 2004, I became an ordained minister with Circle Sanctuary. I wanted my Unitarian Universalist tradition to be what guided my heart, head, and hands personally so that I could be in service to the traditions of the Earth. It affirmed over twenty-five years of volunteer work I had already done.

Being of service to others in Paganism, while holding dear the Purposes of Unitarian Universalism, feeds my soul so that I can give to others. As a Unitarian Universalist who chose to become a Pagan minister, I could bring the practice of deep listening and compassion that I had learned in the pews on Sundays to interfaith settings at various church events and interfaith-council meetings. As a minister I could take a stand for the transformation that can happen when people work together, listen, and engage in dialogue. I am learning that the training of a priestess and minister are the same, and that it has been and will continue to be a lifelong experience.

Today I serve in prison systems on Pagan sabbats to lead services and go to local hospitals as a volunteer chaplain when needed. I participate in interfaith affairs in my community and serve with the Ambassadors to the Parliament of the World's Religions, learning more and more about deep listening and dialogue on an international and interfaith level. I also serve with Pagans in the UUA in various projects and organizations, and in Circle Sanctuary as a minister, teacher, and trainer supporting the ministries there.

Something bigger still drives me, though: my faith. I will always be a bridge and a stand for the people and the home we call Earth to be treated fairly, and for the first Principle of our living tradition in *honoring the inherent worth and dignity of every person.*"

Like that young girl who sat along the river's edge, feeling the energies and love of something bigger than herself, I embrace the sixth Source of our denomination that invites people to honor the *"spiritual teachings of Earth-centered traditions which celebrate the sacred circle of life and instruct us to live in harmony with the rhythms of nature."*

Love is the Spirit in me, and service is my prayer. Thus do I covenant with the God and Goddess.

-◄o►-

JERRIE KISHPAUGH HILDEBRAND *serves on the board of trustees of CUUPS. She is an ordained minister with Circle Sanctuary in Wisconsin and attends First Church Unitarian in Salem, Massachusetts. She is an advisor for the Lady Liberty League, which supports Pagans around issues related to religious freedom and civil rights. She has written articles on Paganism for numerous publications.*

CAKES FOR THE QUEEN OF HEAVEN

SHIRLEY ANN RANCK

Do you not see what they do in the cities of Judah and in the streets of Jerusalem? The children gather wood and the fathers kindle the fire, and the women knead the dough to make cakes to the Queen of Heaven.

(Jeremiah 7:17–18)

As for the word that you have spoken to us in the name of Yahweh—we shall not listen to you. But we shall without fail do everything as we said: we shall burn incense to the Queen of Heaven, and shall pour her libations as we used to do . . . in the cities of Judah, in the streets of Jerusalem. For then we had plenty of food, and we were all well and saw no evil. But since we ceased burning incense to the Queen of Heaven and to pour her libations, we have wanted everything and have been consumed by sword and famine.

(Jeremiah 44:16–18)

In 1986 the Unitarian Universalist Association published a ten-session course I had written called *Cakes for the Queen of Heaven*. It was developed as one way of implementing the UUA's 1977 Women and Religion resolution. Rev. Leslie Westbrook and later Elizabeth Anastos served as editors. The idea was to provide curriculum materials concerning the role of the female in pre-patriarchal religion as well as the presence of strong women in the history of Judaism and Christianity. We decided early on that one course could not cover the presence of goddesses and the role of women in traditions all over the world. We limited this course to the religions of the Ancient Near East, Greece, Rome, the very ancient archeaological discoveries of Old Europe, and a few of the strong women in Judaism and Christianity.

We also decided that to empower women the course had to be personal. We wanted women to have very personal experiences with their religious history. The sessions therefore are both intellectual and experiential, using small-group discussion, crayons, clay, and visualizations to explore the relationship between that history and the personal issues that arise in women living in this patriarchal society. Women struggle with issues of body image, troubled mother-daughter relationships, sexual freedom, and access to power. We needed to know that there was a time when the female body was sacred; that there once was a long-lasting religion in which the chief divine actors were a mother and her daughter; that in very ancient times women had significant power in their societies; that although patriarchal societies have oppressed women for centuries, there have always been strong and talented women. Our female history had been erased and trivialized for too long. In *Cakes*, women would meet ancient goddesses as well as real women in ancient Sumer, in Greece, in Judaism, and in Christianity.

In *Cakes*, we learn that in much of the ancient world, over the course of millennia the Great Goddess was worshipped in three separate aspects: as the maiden, the mother, and the crone. The three aspects of the Goddess were linked to the phases of the moon—the waxing moon was the maiden with all her possibilities, the full moon was the abundance of the mother, and the waning moon was the wisdom of the old woman. Women felt in their own bodies and menstrual cycles a very close connection with the phases of the moon and the cycles of birth, growth, and death that they saw in the plants and animals around them.

Women were thought to be endowed with divine power because they could bleed without harm, give birth to new life, and provide milk. Menstrual blood was sacred and thought to contain the divine wisdom that created new human beings. People believed that when a woman stopped bleeding she was storing and retaining that divine wisdom.

Another way of describing the triple Goddess was as creator, preserver, and destroyer. In this rendition the crone takes on not only wisdom but also the power of death. She is the one who knows when an individual life must end in order for new life to begin. She is the Goddess of that mysterious transformation that occurs as we are returned to the Earth, to the ongoing cycle of life and death. In the old Goddess religions death was believed to be part of the cycle of life.

In later times myths tell us that male deities waged battles against the Goddess, tricked her into giving up her power or, if she was very powerful, married her. If the myths of a culture reflect its social arrangements, women must have suffered an overall loss of power and respect. Mythology tells us that in early historic times goddesses and gods reigned together with varying amounts of power. Eventually the male deities became the chief deities. In Judaism and Christianity the male God became the only deity.

Cakes also explores what happened to the old religion when the patriarchal deities came into power. Some say that the old religions of the Western world survived in secret as Witchcraft. Christianity was often imposed on the city people by a king or ruler who had been converted. To the country people, the Pagans (from the Latin *Paganus*, or country person), the new religion seemed familiar: a mother and her divine child who dies and is reborn. They continued to practice the old religion. As the feudal system crumbled, however, the stability of the medieval Christian church was shaken and could tolerate no rivals.

In 1484 the Papal Bull of Innocent VII turned the Inquisition against the old religion. The *Malleus Malleficarum*, or *Hammer of the Witches*, was published in 1486, and a reign of terror began in Europe that lasted into the eighteenth century. Every unspeakable torture was inflicted to obtain "confessions." Many thousands of people (80 percent of them women) were burned at the stake. The old religion of the Goddess was driven underground.

If we accept the theory that myths reflect the power structures of societies, it follows that women had significant power in the early history of humanity but had that power wrested away in a long struggle. The big question, of course, is why? Many theories have been suggested to explain this shift in power. These theories are presented and discussed in *Cakes*. The important fact here is that women lost power in the ancient Western world, and needed to reclaim it in creative ways in today's world.

To open and close each session I suggested that groups light a candle and read a poem or sing a song related to the session. I encouraged women to bring their own readings or songs or pictures to share. At the time I thought it was just a good way to provide a clear beginning and ending for each session. As a Humanist I did not think to call these techniques ritual. But in these *Cakes* study groups women began to create altars and to design elaborate and meaningful rites to express their experiences. A deep and widespread hunger for rituals relevant to modern life was discovered.

In churches where the course was offered year after year to more and more women and men, ritual and worship began to reflect the personal and global issues of our own day: How shall women and men relate to each other as equals? How shall we in our ethnic diversity learn to respect each other? How can we come together to halt the destruction of our environment? How can we honor the sacredness of our lives and the Earth?

An unexpected but very timely learning was that the old religions also honored the Earth. Gaia (Earth), perhaps the oldest of the Greek deities, is celebrated by the poet Homer. He wrote this, as translated by Hugh G. Evelyn-White:

> I will sing of the well-founded Earth, mother of all,
>   eldest of all beings
> She feeds all creatures that are in the world,
> all that go upon the goodly land,
> and all that are in the paths of the seas, and all that fly:
> all these are fed of her store.
> Through you, O queen, [people] are blessed in their
>   children
> and blessed in their harvests,
> and to you it belongs to give means of life . . .
> O Holy Goddess, bountiful spirit.
> Hail, Mother of the gods, wife of starry Heaven;
> freely bestow upon me for this my song substance that
>   cheers the heart!

Pagans celebrated the phases of the moon, the solstices, the spring and fall equinoxes. They seemed to feel a real connection with the natural world. Such celebrations were not written into the *Cakes* course but were added as many groups saw in these old Pagan customs some answers to our ecological crisis. In some of our congregations women, after using the *Cakes* course, taught it to groups that included men. Men as well as women began to reclaim our ancient Pagan Earth-centered traditions.

Many of the changes in our UU congregations over the past thirty years can be traced at least in part to the influence of women and men who took the *Cakes* course. Perhaps the most significant and visible change is the strong emergence of women as ordained ministers. Women now comprise more than fifty percent of our clergy.

Another change is that the personal has become more and more important in sermons, in special services, and in the increasing number of small group activities. Members not only attend Sunday services and serve on committees; they also meet in small groups to meditate, to share the joys and sorrows of their personal lives, or to be advocates for social justice in their communities. For many the purpose of religion is no longer how to escape to a better supernatural realm after death, but rather how best to honor life in this natural world "of which we are a part," to quote the seventh Principle.

We also have more and more services and celebrations of the seasons—solstices, equinoxes, the phases of the moon. We honor death in the fall, new life in the spring. Drumming and chanting drawn from Pagan and Earth-centered traditions are often heard in these services and celebrations. New songs and chants and readings expressing Pagan or

Earth-centered views are now included in our hymnal. Religious education materials celebrating women and the Earth have been created for adults and children.

Also interesting are the ways in which we rational scientific humanists, as well as our theists, have reclaimed ritual. Women have created new rituals to mark the stages of their lives as maiden, mother, and crone. In many places we have rearranged the furniture in our sanctuaries so that we sit or stand in concentric or half circles. In the center we sometimes create a beautiful altar with flowers and candles and mementos of loved ones who have died, expressing the Earth-centered view that they are still part of our Earthly community. Or the center may be used for a special dance involving everyone as they celebrate a season. Spiral dances are especially popular. In addition to lighting a chalice to begin a service, there is often a special honoring of the elements of the natural world—air, fire, water, and Earth.

Cakes for the Queen of Heaven was effective not only in implementing the Women and Religion resolution, but also in giving expression to our growing concern for the Earth.

Rise Up & Call Her Name

Elizabeth Fisher

A multicultural feminist thealogy course, *Rise Up & Call Her Name: A Woman-Honoring Journey into Global Earth-Based Spiritualities,* explores perspectives encompassing multiple Pagan components. It is a companion to the curriculum *Cakes for the Queen of Heaven,* written by Rev. Shirley Ranck, who made this comment about *Rise Up* in her memoir *The Grandmother Galaxy*: "It was a great pleasure to me to see that these issues of respect for the Earth, of ritual, our ancestors, and of darkness which were not addressed directly in *Cakes* were brought dramatically into our awareness in *Rise Up & Call Her Name.*"

Both programs are expressions of the Women and Religion resolution passed unanimously at the 1977 General Assembly. The author of the resolution, Lucile Schuck Longview, was also deeply committed to Earth-honoring practices, as were many of those responsible for launching the UU women's movement. The early convocations in 1979 and 1980 featured rituals that called out the elements of Earth, air, fire, and water, and upheld ecological principles. This was a cutting-edge perspective in UU circles back then.

The particular form of spirituality embodied in *Rise Up* takes a global perspective that honors the diverse roots of a variety of spiritual beliefs and practices. While valuing all genders, *Rise Up* centers on rituals, symbols, and images that provide affirmative action for the female divine in her many shapes and colors. Believing it is important to honor the real-life circumstances in locations around the world, this spiritual journey includes cultural sensitivity information that supports social justice for all.

A mix of intellectual and artistic activities, rich visuals, music, conversation, and creative ritual makes up the sessions. *Cakes* established this structure; *Rise Up* greatly expanded it. Collaboration for me is a central tenet of UU Pagan practice, and it was an essential element in the creation of this program. Scores of contributions from varied sources are woven into its lush fabric.

So, what was going on in the larger culture in the 1960s, 1970s, and 1980s that called for the creation of these programs? Are they still relevant today? How did they affect Unitarian Universalism?

As many of us recall and others have heard, those decades were periods that found society in flux, conflict, and deep anxiety. There was a desire for understanding and new perspectives, which stimulated a significant number of individuals to seek avenues to personal authenticity and racial reconciliations.

In the 1960s, Western monotheistic religions were being scrutinized for the absence of respect for nature in their teachings and activities. The concerns about the destruction of ecological systems Rachel Carson raised in *Silent Spring* (1962) were for many people spiritual as well as scientific. In addition, forced segregation, racial prejudice, and sexism were challenged. Unitarian Universalists were at the forefront of taking on these issues then as we are today.

My own story begins in the 1950s and 60s. I grew up living in northern Ohio next to a large wooded park where I spent hours walking my dog and feeling at home among trees and canyons. I attended a liberal Congregational church during my youth and was interested in ethics. In my Christian Sunday-school classes, I developed an ethical outlook that valued caring, sharing, and compassion, which has allowed me to appreciate the various interpretations of Christianity.

I was bothered, however, by the Christian concept of divinity, which seemed to be a hierarchical concept: God over all creation. I was attracted rather to the phrase "God is within you," except that it seemed to me God was in everything. The pronoun *he* was the only one used to describe the all-powerful. My mother and father were feminists of sorts, encouraging me to believe girls deserved as much consideration and opportunity as boys. So why not use the pronoun *she* when describing the divine?

After earning a degree in psychology with a minor in history and English from the University of Michigan in 1969, I was well aware of the absence of women in both positions of authority and academic focus. The female voice and story was anemic at best, although I sensed that was about to change.

During my college days I did, however, make one helpful discovery that foretold my future endeavors. I took a class on Oriental religions, which included brief mentions of Kuan Yin, a compassionate female deity revered throughout Asia. In the early 1970s, I moved to California, which gave me access to Asian communities, where I attended many educational events and seasonal festivals where this goddess was at the center. I felt called to go much deeper into a spiritual practice focused on this female divinity whose expressed purpose is to "hear the cries of the world."

Instinctively, I formed a personal connection to her that continued to expand. I read about her whenever I had the opportunity. I collected statues of her and visited shrines that contained her image. As I explored other cultures, I found equally empowering female deities who opened my heart and mind.

In the early 1980s, I began attending services at the San Francisco Unitarian Society. I learned that at every institutional level of the denomination there were many energetic women and men who shared my passions for the sacredness of nature, feminist spirituality, and social justice. I felt at home and joined.

Soon I met Shirley Ranck at a district Women and Religion meeting and learned about the course she had recently written. In 1984, I arranged for her to teach *Cakes* at the San Francisco Church to an enthusiastic response. Having just returned from serving as parish minister in Cincinnati, she was deeply committed to getting the UUA's final approval to publish *Cakes*. Participants in the class wrote letters of support to her editor. Needless to say, *Cakes* was published (in 1986) and has become an honored source of both information and inspiration.

Following the publication of *Cakes*, the UU Women's Federation (UUWF) undertook a survey of its members, thousands at that time, asking what resources they were most interested in having provided. The answer was: more materials about woman-honoring, Earth-based spirituality. Because I was the co-convener of my district's Women and Religion Task Force and had taught *Cakes*, I was asked by the UUWF board to be a speaker on a panel at the General Assembly in Palm Springs in 1988 entitled "*Cakes*, Well-Done or Half-Baked?" I was on the well-done side, testifying how this program had changed my life, while advocating for additional programming that covered areas not included in *Cakes*. Shirley was the first to acknowledge that one program cannot cover everything.

The testimony from the large audience was telling. Many claimed the program had changed their lives as well, and they wanted to magnify what had been set into motion. This included requests for more cross-cultural material, creative ritual opportunities, thealogical perspectives dealing with racist and sexist religious concepts, and hands-on activities.

This session, coupled with my discovery of so many female deities worldwide, drew me to propose what became *Rise Up*. These goddesses had so enriched my spiritual life and my sense of well-being that I wanted to share them with others. Judging from the feedback I have received over the last twenty years, many who have taken *Rise Up* also feel this connection and their impact.

Shirley Ranck enthusiastically supported my idea and my role in leading the project. Lucile Longview, whom I had met in 1985, helped me to get in touch with the UUWF board and present my idea. She saw it as an important next step in implementing the Women and Religion resolution. In 1989, the UUWF sponsored a grant application for my proposal to the Fund for Unitarian Universalism, which was approved. Another grant was awarded in 1992 to provide training for the program's facilitators.

As Shirley pointed out, there are important areas of *Rise Up* that expand *Cakes*. Together these two courses reinforced perspectives that are also found in UU Paganism. They are credited with playing a significant role in the adoption of the Sixth source into the UUA Principles at General Assembly in 1995.

Now, a few examples of what went on behind the scenes. When creating *Rise Up*, I held extended conversations with several women from diverse backgrounds. They prepared statements that were recorded for the course, taking all of us beyond the racial divide. These are incredibly valuable since this type of exchange is rare in our society, even today. We are often too guarded to speak our truth.

I am deeply grateful to these women for their willingness to share from their hearts. Many participants reported feeling enriched by these firsthand renditions, which connect Earth-honoring perspectives with real-life realities. This kind of opportunity is what makes Unitarian Universalism a living tradition.

My own interest in breaking through racial segregation began in my youth. Growing up in a suburban white-only environment, I felt isolated from the rich histories I only heard about through reading and a few movies. I learned a bit of African-American social history, mostly from literature. The segregation of the North into inner city and suburb, and the racial tensions of the South playing out on the television made it clear there was a lot that wasn't being discussed.

As I continued to explore religious traditions, I began to read extensively about the Earth-based aspects of African-American culture and what African-American women thought was important about their own cultures. I discovered close relationships to the natural world were common in African-American experiences in rural areas.

I worked with several African-American women to develop sections of *Rise Up*. One woman in particular, Betty Reid Soskin, stands out. Betty was actively involved in Unitarian Universalism over decades, including serving on the board of trustees of Starr King School for the Ministry.

I chose to feature her story and her African-American music and bookstore, which she owned and operated for many years, because it represented the wide range of black culture. Betty herself identified as a Humanist with an appreciation for the natural world.

We spent countless hours sorting out what was happening between white and black people and how the chasm could be bridged. These discussions produced suggestions for ways participants could open up conversations about race in their local communities, encouraging firsthand exchanges that can lead to lasting alliances.

Many years later, Betty became an employee of the National Park System when she was eighty-five years old. She was instrumental in shaping the Rosie the Riveter/ World War II Home Front National Historical Park in Richmond, California. She ensured the complete history was told, successfully advocating for the full disclosure of the racism of that period. Betty's authenticity and her desire to share have made her a national spokesperson for the African-American experience.

Several other African-American Unitarian Universalists and others who had interest in African-based religions contributed their insights, knowledge, and experiences. For example, they helped me grasp the spiritual significance of "improvisation," which is especially important in African-American quilting, widespread among women from early slave days to the present.

Another deeply important exchange for me shaped an important section of this course. I grew up with a respect for Native American culture. We learned about the lifestyles of the local tribes but little about the lives of native women. In my early explorations, I discovered in the library a few texts on Native American outlooks, which included female images such as Spider Woman, who "sings the world into being." These references stayed with me, ripened, and eventually found their expression in *Rise Up & Call Her Name*.

During development, I met Anpetu Winyan, a Lakota pipe woman who shared many important elements of her culture and sacred practices with me. Some of these she allowed to be included. I learned about the circumstances of Native Americans across the continent, and Native Hawaiians too. *Rise Up* includes stories, art, and wisdom from a range of these peoples.

I wondered whether we were appropriating when we incorporated their practices into our creative rituals. For me, distinguishing between appropriation and appreciation resolves this concern. Appreciation is built on true knowing, which requires experience and not mere observation.

I consulted with Anpetu about what would best reflect her culture. She recommended honoring the Four Directions through poetry, as well as cleansing sacred space with sage, thereby providing both experience and information. Many who have experienced *Rise Up* have benefitted from her written and spoken pieces, art activities, and ceremonial knowledge that are included in the curriculum. These contributions have strengthened Unitarian Universalist commitment to the survival of indigenous peoples and expanded respect for Native-American beliefs and perspectives.

So, have these two curricula, *Cakes for the Queen of Heaven* and *Rise Up & Call Her Name*, exerted influence outside Unitarian Universalist circles? The answer is a resounding yes. I have heard from scholars teaching in a prominent women's spirituality program that draws students from all over the world that many of their students first discovered the range and depth of Goddess- and women-honoring spirituality from these two courses.

These programs have convened in bookshops, community centers, retreats, and temples, and used by other denominations successfully. Musical pieces, ceremonies, and concepts that are included in these two curriculum programs show up in public gatherings from coast to coast. Aspects are incorporated in passage-of-life celebrations of a girl's first menses to an older woman's croning.

Last year *Rise Up*'s twentieth anniversary was celebrated by those who had attended the class at the Unitarian Universalist Church of Berkeley in 1995, and who are still meeting together. This small-group bonding has occurred in many locations. Many of those who have never had the experience of these courses still reaped their benefits, as the content and processes of the courses have been incorporated into congregational services, forums, and spiritual sharing circles.

In the last fifty years, there has been a profound paradigm shift in attitudes toward the Earth. Our advocacy for the sacredness of our beautiful blue-green planet has been widely felt. The incorporation of Earth-honoring perspectives into Unitarian Universalism and the ongoing contributions of Pagan-identified people have supported this important change. And, thanks to the commitment of so many who have facilitated groups and shared resources, more and more people each day come to appreciate the female divine in all her glorious shapes and colors.

◄o►

ELIZABETH FISHER *is the author of the UU Women's Federation course* Rise Up & Call Her Name: A Woman-Honoring Journey into Global Earth-based Spiritualties *and the UU Service Committee's* Gender Justice: Women's Rights are Human Rights. *She curates a website (LucilesRedNotebook.org) on the origins and impact of the UU Women and Religion Movement and writes on UU Paganism for the Patheos Blog "Nature's Path." See www.RiseUpandCallHerName.com.*

A Difference of
Just a Few Words

Paul L'Herrou

Sometime during the early months of 1984, I received, as did all Unitarian Universalist ministers, a packet of materials sent from the headquarters of the Unitarian Universalist Association. It contained the proposed wording for the new Principles section of Article II: Principles & Purposes of the Bylaws of the Unitarian Universalist Association.

The original 1961 statement of Principles had been crafted as a statement of common understanding at the time of the merger of the Universalist Church of America and the American Unitarian Association to form the Unitarian Universalist Association. Over time, it had become increasingly apparent that the original Principles and Purposes had become hopelessly out of date and Unitarian Universalism was outgrowing what was our major statement of religious identity. In particular, the statement of Principles represented a masculine worldview for a religious movement which was moving in the direction of sexual and gender equality as well as beginning to recognize and affirm the naturally vast diversity of gender and sexual expression.

The major energy that eventually led to the creation of the new statement came from Unitarian Universalist women who sought greater gender equality within the denomination. As with all efforts to bring about positive change, it was a struggle to make headway against the status quo. At long last, a denominational committee was formed and tasked to create wording to replace the original statement of Principles. The committee's work resulted in a proposal to replace the original statement of Principles with seven newly written Principles. These were to be followed by a list of five Sources, from which our religious tradition draws. The sixth Source—"Spiritual teachings of Earth-centered traditions which celebrate the sacred circle of life and instruct us to live in harmony with the rhythms of nature"—was added later, and did not appear in early editions of the hymn book *Singing the Living Tradition*.

The proposed wording of Principles and Sources was to be presented for a vote of the delegates at the Unitarian Universalist Association's 1984 General Assembly in Columbus, Ohio. I had been anxiously anticipating receipt of the proposed new wording, because from that time forward it would serve as the defining statement of Unitarian Universalism.

As I read the proposed wording of the Principles, I was excited to see that the committee had managed to incorporate so well the major qualities, the strong principles that shape our movement and which are so very important to us as Unitarian Universalists. That is, until I reached the Seventh Principle! I read "respect for Earth and interdependence of its living systems," and my excitement drained away.

The first thing that struck me about the wording was that it asked us to care about something outside of ourselves. This is the problem with much charity and abstract social action. We want to be helpful, so we give money or food or a little of our time, but we don't identify with the needy or feel ownership of all those problems out there. I had come to believe that it was only when we feel the hunger of those who lack adequate food or the fear of those whose lives are caught in the crossfire of war or feel the deep personal loss of a bulldozed rainforest that we go beyond a modest donation of money or time and really become engaged.

At that time I had been studying deep ecology, an environmental philosophy that originated with the insights of Norwegian philosopher Arne Næss in 1973. The philosophy of deep ecology values all living beings, regardless of their relative value or benefit to us or their perceived level of higher or lower consciousness. It is holistic in that it sees all beings, including us, as part of one diverse and complex reality within which all creatures are interdependent.

My view of human relations and ethics had also been challenged and changed by feminist thealogy, with its emphasis on human interdependence and mutual caring and the sacredness of interrelationship. In particular, I had become very aware of the work of Carol Gilligan, which challenged the prevailing masculine perspective that assumed morality and ethics must be based on abstract principles. Gilligan showed that many women, particularly at that time, based their ethical and moral decisions on the living structure of interdependent human relationships.

Two perspectives pointed to the same integral dynamic. Gilligan's work showed that reliable guidelines for human inter-relating can better be found within the intrinsic quality of humanness as opposed to abstracted principles. Deep ecology showed that grounding for our relationship to nature is best found in our intrinsic position and inter-relationship within the natural world.

I had also come to see that the natural world is made up of more than what we think of as "living systems." We have also to take into account the non-living—all that is gaseous, liquid, solid, or perhaps in transition from one state to another. For instance, we usually think of a sandy beach as non-living. However, a beach is an eco-system made up of sand and water, crabs and clams, grasses and microscopic flora and fauna, wind and waves and tides, all relating interdependently. The tides also remind us that the Earth, sun, moon, and actually everything in the universe exists in an interdependent relationship.

In addition, I had hoped to find a philological or theological statement that would support my personal spirituality. I trace my own spiritual awakening to an article about

George Nakashima, which I had stumbled upon much earlier. Nakashima was an architect, woodworker, and creator of beautiful and unique furniture. Before reading that article, I had never imagined that someone, when he was ready to create a new piece of furniture, would wander among slabs of tree trunks until he felt that a particular slab of wood spoke to him. He then applied his skills of craftsmanship and creativity to enable the tree's "yearning to live again" as a useful and uniquely beautiful work of art. Since then, I have read his writings, searched out pieces of his furniture in the collection of the Museum of Fine Arts, Boston, and visited his workshop, now run by his daughter, in New Hope, Pennsylvania. His deep connections to *The Soul of a Tree*, as he titled his book, has inspired my own Earth-centered spiritual exploration.

My love for Earth-centered spirituality is cultivated by my connection to nature, which is a source of grounding in my life. It is important to me that this spirituality be aligned with the real world. The spiritual traditions referenced in the sixth Source remind us that we human beings have emerged from and evolved within the real-world workings of nature. We are natural beings (though we often fail to act as such). I find spiritual nurture and grounding in the natural world I see around me. The entire natural world is interdependent, whether we think only in terms of ecology—the study of the interrelationship of Earth-bound organisms and their environments—or in terms of the workings of the solar system, holding us within the

Milky Way galaxy, which in turn is held by forces within the entire cosmos.

As I struggled to define how I would have wanted this proposed seventh Principle to read, it became clear to me that, for any such statement to have any real depth, it must apply not only to our environmental vision, but also to our human relations, and must necessarily be grounded in an articulation of a basic and underlying principle.

I also drew upon the web imagery used in the well-known speech attributed to Chief Seattle. I have since learned, however, that the original translator of Seattle's speech into English was not very reliable, and the words as we currently know them were probably crafted by a television writer, who was apparently influenced by process theologian Bernard Loomer. So the final wording may have inadvertently been influenced by Loomer's theology, though I was not aware of it at the time.

In any case, I went to the General Assembly at the Ohio State University campus in Columbus, Ohio, carrying with me the basic words I planned to propose as an amendment. During the first few days at the General Assembly I shared my version with several close colleagues, seeking to tap their wisdom as I attempted to improve upon and polish the language, but not change its substance.

The time came when the work of the committee was presented and a motion was put on the floor for the new proposed Principles and Sources. The new wording had been widely discussed in advance and so did not draw very much discussion by the delegates. They were ready to vote to accept the entire package. I then rose and, with some trepidation, asked if an amendment would be in order. I recall hearing several groans from the delegates who were ready to vote and move on without further discussion. The moderator said that an amendment would be in order at that time. I moved to substitute the new wording for the seventh Principle. I recall that at first there was sort of a questioning attitude by the assembly, but after some brief discussion, the wording, the difference of just a few words, really—"Respect for the interdependent web of all existence of which we are part"—was overwhelmingly accepted.

The assembly then moved almost unanimously to accept the work of the committee, including the amended words for the seventh Principle. Any change to the bylaws of the UUA requires a second affirmative vote at the subsequent General Assembly. The following year, 1985, there was little or no significant discussion or dissent, and the new Principles and Sources became (with the subsequent addition of the sixth Source) our guiding document.

It has often been pointed out that the seventh Principle, together with the First Principle ("The inherent worth and dignity of every person"), undergird our human relationships in ways that lead us to oppose the forces of oppression and affirm democratic forms of governance. Together, these two Principles resolve the inherent conflict between the individual and the group. Together they support the search for truth and meaning and the quest for world peace.

What had begun as an attempt to craft a more adequate ecological statement grew into a much more encompassing philosophical, theological, and spiritual statement. In a culture that is becoming increasingly individualistic, the seventh Principle offers an opposing vision, one of grounding ourselves in community and human relationship as well as in the natural world. In this way it transcends our tendency toward egotistical self-centeredness and leads us to seek a spiritual and emotional foundation beyond our limited selves. When we are grounded, not just by searching within, but in connecting to the strands that connect us to all existence, we are challenged to reach out to protect the environment and promote justice for all.

In his "Letter from a Birmingham Jail," Martin Luther King Jr. used similar imagery to challenge the white clergy of Birmingham:

> I am cognizant of the interrelatedness of all communities and states. I cannot sit idly by in Atlanta and not be concerned about what happens in Birmingham. Injustice anywhere is a threat to justice everywhere. We are caught in an inescapable network of mutuality, tied in a single garment of destiny. Whatever affects one directly, affects all indirectly.

The quality of interdependence seems to be woven throughout the ultimate nature of reality. Traditional theists and those seeking connections with a higher power may find the interdependent web to be an essential facet of the

Ultimate. Buddhists and other non-theists and atheists may find in the interdependent web an understanding of the world that transcends us and leads our lives to purpose, meaning, and greater spiritual growth. Seekers of the sacred through Goddess imagery and Pagan traditions, as well as Native American and other Earth-centered spiritual seekers, will recognize the interdependent web as a familiar quality of a feminist and Earth-centered spirituality. Although I do not personally identify as a Unitarian Universalist Pagan, my own spiritual roots are indeed watered, as the sixth Source reads, by the "spiritual teachings of Earth-centered traditions which celebrate the sacred circle of life and instruct us to live in harmony with the rhythms of nature."

We each travel our own unique path as we experience life and seek to give our lives meaning and purpose, to ground our actions and decisions in the larger reality, and to nurture our beings through a sense of reverence and awe. The interdependent web opens our hearts to a broader experience of and a deeper concern for the larger world and also holds and supports us in times of difficulty, loss, and grief. The interdependent web provides a very real and yet transcendent grounding and perspective for our individual life journeys.

-◄o►-

PAUL L'HERROU *is retired and lives in Columbus, Ohio, with his wife and colleague, Sylvia Howe. Ordained in 1974, L'Herrou served Unitarian Universalist churches as settled minister, as co-minister with Sylvia Howe, and as an accredited interim minister. He retired in 2007 and both of them are now active lay members of the First Unitarian Universalist Church of Columbus.*

Thirty Years of CUUPS

David Pollard

One of the great things about Earth-centered spirituality, which includes the modern Pagan movement and a bit more, is its ability to respond to a changing environment. While other faith traditions may primarily be in relationship with an unchanging text, or the history of a specific people, we are in relationship with the world as it is. We are in relationship with the outside world—with its endangered species and fracked watersheds—as well as the world as it is within ourselves, as we engage ourselves and each other in working toward a less patriarchal, less racist, more sustainable future.

The way we engage each other to create this greater beloved community is through ritual. For most Pagans this is the first response to a difficult situation, in the same way that Christians seek the solace of prayer, Buddhists meditate, and Humanists seek an education in the underlying facts. I've been told that this *drive for ritual* is what first got people together to form the Covenant of Unitarian Universalist Pagans (CUUPS).

At the 1985 UUA General Assembly in Atlanta, a handful of UU seminary students, including Lesley Phillips, Linda Pinti, and Christa Landon, circulated a flyer for a meeting of people who wanted to provide summer solstice or midsummer rituals for future General Assemblies. A couple dozen people gathered and passed around a notepad to collect addresses. They agreed that having rituals at future General Assemblies was both laudable and feasible and came up with the name of their new organization.

If the need for ritual was the spark that started CUUPS, graduates of the UU religious education course *Cakes for the Queen of Heaven* were the kindling. At the time, this was a brand-new course by Rev. Shirley Ranck, introducing the idea of the divine feminine and the goddesses of classical antiquity to thousands of UU women. CUUPS provided *Cakes* graduates a framework to continue their ritual work within a supportive environment.

Another way to educate Unitarian Universalists about Paganism was through hosting programming at the UUA's annual General Assemblies. So, throughout the 1990s, CUUPS hosted a who's who of Pagan and Goddess-oriented guest speakers, like Margot Adler, Starhawk, Selena Fox, Luisha Teish, Andra Corbin, Charlene Spretnak, and Brook Medicine Eagle, as well as a few Christian scholars who were knowledgeable about the modern Pagan movement, like Harvey Cox and Rosemary Radford Ruether. Margot

Adler joined the CUUPS board early on, then joined a UU congregation in 1991. Starhawk spoke to several hundred people at a General Assembly, drawing an audience from far beyond the Pagan contingent. Nearly all of these programs were recorded onto cassette tapes and sold through the CUUPS newsletter, *Pagan NUUS*.

These outreach efforts first got me involved with CUUPS. In 1990, as a young adult and a Unitarian Universalist for less than two years, I was also the incoming president for my fellowship. The fellowship sent me to the General Assembly, and I got to feed my inner Pagan in ways I never even envisioned in my home congregation. I got to prostrate myself before religious statuary (although this was in a UU Buddhist service, not a Pagan one) and attend an ornate offering prayer service in a foreign language (via the International Association for Religious Freedom's morning Shinto prayer service). These were things I didn't feel I could bring home with me. But then I found CUUPS. I knew there were members at my home fellowship who were interested in goddesses and Wicca. CUUPS offered resources that I could use at home!

While this was taking place, CUUPS was deeply involved in an effort to amend the UUA Principles and Purposes to explicitly include Earth-centered spiritualty as a primary source of Unitarian Universalist faith. This required an amendment to the UUA bylaws, which entailed approval votes at two consecutive General Assemblies, the final vote requiring a two-thirds majority. If at any time in the process the proposed amendment was modified, the process had to start over from scratch. So what began as a proposal to the Massachusetts Bay District Annual Meeting in 1990 did not become complete until its final approval vote of 735–358 at the 1995 UUA General Assembly in Spokane, Washington. The shepherding of this proposal through its rather complicated path to final adoption was a major focus for CUUPS leadership in the first half of the 1990s. Because of this, our sixth Source now includes "spiritual teachings of Earth-centered traditions which celebrate the sacred circle of life and instruct us to live in harmony with the rhythms of nature."

This was not just a CUUPS effort. There was overwhelming support and coordination from the youth and young adult affiliates, the Seventh Principle Project (now known as UU Ministry for Earth), the UU Women's Federation and UU Women in Religion organizations, UUs for Native and Indigenous Affairs, and many others.

The next batch of changes to CUUPS came through the Internet and the way its members chose to use it. In the early days of CUUPS, most communications between members and chapters were done through our newsletter, which only came out three to four times per year. Email and mailing lists allowed members and chapters to contact each other directly, allowing them to share ritual scripts and brainstorm about problems they had with their home congregations. Unfortunately, CUUPS Continental was very hesitant to jump onto the Internet, as were local chapters, which often operated twelve months a year. CUUPS leadership focused instead on preparing for and running pro-gramming for General Assembly in June and convocations in the fall. CUUPS finances couldn't support a full-time staff at anything near a living wage, and the board at the time was comprised of people who had little, if any, computer experience. They had to focus on other areas, including getting the sixth Source passed.

The year following final adoption of the sixth Source, the founding co-chairs of CUUPS, Linda Pinti and Lesley Phillips, turned over the reins of the organization to a new generation, which included me. We attempted to bring CUUPS into closer connection to its network of chapters scattered across the United States, and in 1999 CUUPS received its largest donation ever, a nationally distributed magazine. *Connections Magazine* was started by Summer and Robin Windsong and it had grown to a quarterly publication that was distributed through most national bookstore chains as well as a large variety of metaphysical bookstores. While it was generating a small profit, it wasn't enough for the two of them to live on, so they donated it to CUUPS with the hope that it would help fund the expansion of UU Paganism and provide a public mouthpiece for not just UU Paganism but Unitarian Universalism as well. For about two years the magazine was the only broadly sold Unitarian Universalist publica-tion available in communities all across North America. Not surprisingly, during this time CUUPS hit its peak paid membership and budget.

Then, when the dot-com bust occurred, not only did advertising sales substantially decline, but our distributor declared bankruptcy, owing CUUPS close to twenty thousand dollars. CUUPS had to cease publication of *Connections*. While there was some interest in bringing it back shortly thereafter, the postage disruptions and massive rate increases after 9/11 and the anthrax scare made it clear this wouldn't be feasible.

CUUPS faced some other challenges in the following years. In 2005 a couple of key board members, our president and secretary, were affected by Hurricanes Katrina and Rita and had to resign from the board with little warning. Shortly after that the UUA announced that it was eliminating the organizational category called Independent Affiliates in which CUUPS and other organizations resided. Unfortunately this was miscommunicated to some as "CUUPS is getting kicked out of the UUA," which resulted in some chapters disbanding. Another effect of this change was that CUUPS no longer had guaranteed programming slots at General Assembly, and after 2006 did not have programs at the UUA General Assembly until our mid-summer celebration ceremony in 2013.

This is where the adaptability of Pagans comes to the fore. Realizing that we no longer had the opportunities to affordably distribute material in print, or through major presentations at General Assembly, CUUPS found a new platform in social media. In late 2007, we started a free email newsletter, which quickly grew to more than three thousand subscribers. A couple years later, CUUPS created a Facebook discussion group, initially to organize against an effort to restate the Principles and Purposes that would eliminate the text of the sixth Source. Later we started a CUUPS Facebook page to serve as the "Wayside Pulpit" of UU Paganism, and it has grown into one of the largest UU pages on the web, with approximately seventeen thousand likes. In 2010, CUUPS started the CUUPS Podcast, which not only provided current events about CUUPS and UU Paganism, but also included recordings from some of the more popular general events from the early years of CUUPS. CUUPS also ran its first sermon contest, in which the listeners of the podcast listened to and judged the finalists.

At the end of 2014, CUUPS reached an agreement with Patheos, an online platform on religion, to create a blog called "Nature's Path." This featured UU Pagan and Earth-centered content for their very active Pagan channel. Ten months later, we were told that it was the fourth-most popular blog out of more than thirty Pagan blogs they host. Most recently, CUUPS has begun re-entering print. We participated in the crowdfunding for John Halstead's *Godless Paganism* anthology, had current and former board members work with Skinner House in the creation of this volume, and are currently investigating publishing an anthology of a selection from the more than two hundred essays on the "Nature's Path" blog.

When the UUA started its pilot program of Covenanting Communities in 2015, CUUPS was the only former Independent Affiliate organization to participate in it. This may be because of our success in reaching out through social media—especially to those who are unchurched but still identify as Unitarian Universalists. The really exciting part of the Covenanting Communities program isn't just how it's inspiring us to adapt further into the future, but also that it indicates that the UUA is willing to adapt as it realizes that there is more to a religious movement than brick-and-mortar churches and centralized support staff. Maybe we're finally starting to rub off on them!

What has kept me actively engaged with CUUPS for most of the last quarter century is that I know that at any time I can throw the phrase *CUUPS* into a search engine and find out that some chapter out there is doing something interesting that I likely haven't heard about before. Because of moving around and changing jobs over the years, I've been part of four different Unitarian Universalist congregations. But even when my home congregation acts in ways I find deeply frustrating, and it feels so easy just to disengage and fade away, I can always fall back on my CUUPS family and stay busy there until my local difficulties have resolved themselves and we can move forward again together. So while I occasionally hear concerns from people saying they are hesitant to recommend CUUPS to their members because they want them to stay active with their neighborhood congregation, my lived experience is that participation with CUUPS and other non-congregational parts of the UU movement actually strengthens and reinforces my congregational life.

—◦—

DAVID POLLARD *is the executive director for CUUPS. He was
also president of CUUPS from 2010 until 2013 and served on
its board. He is a member of Pathways Church in Hurst, Texas,
where he is currently president of the board of trustees and has
also been actively involved with North Texas UU Congregation
for much of the past two decades.*

CHANGING UNITARIAN UNIVERSALIST THEA/OLOGY

SHIRLEY ANN RANCK

Scientists are developing a growing respect for all living things, and have discovered that cooperation with nature rather than ruling over it leads to humanity's larger good.
—*Sophia Fahs*

We, the member congregations of the Unitarian Universalist Association, covenant to affirm and promote . . . respect for the interdependent web of all existence of which we are a part.
—*UUA seventh Principle*

The living tradition we share draws from many sources including . . . spiritual teachings of Earth-centered traditions which celebrate the sacred circle of life and instruct us to live in harmony with the rhythms of nature.
—*UUA sixth Source*

Perhaps the most important religious task of our time has been learning to take pluralism seriously. It has been necessary for each of us to begin to see our own tradition as one among many and to understand that no one tradition has the whole truth. Such pluralism cuts across all the boundaries of race, nationality, and gender. In the words of Luisah Teish's poem "Multicolored Mama":

> I will not wear
> your narrow racial jackets
> as the blood of many nations
> runs sweetly thru my veins.

In the nineteenth century, Ralph Waldo Emerson and the young Theodore Parker declared, as summarized by Conrad Wright in *Walking Together*, that "religion is not a matter of proof from the evidence of historical events, but is grounded on the inner religious consciousness." They insisted that Christianity was true only to the extent that it authentically expressed a universal religious impulse that all religious people share. Universal, extending beyond even the boundaries of Christianity.

In the twentieth century Sophia Fahs made important contributions to our awareness of other traditions. Her book *Beginnings of Earth and Sky*, a collection of creation stories from around the world, was published in 1938. It includes the biblical creation story as one among many. Her book *From Long Ago and Many Lands*, another collection of religious stories from around the world, was first published in 1948.

Pluralism, however, is not just about people. Postmodern scientists have taught us that we are connected in myriad ways to all of life. As Fahs writes in *Today's Children, Yesterday's Heritage*,

> We live in one world where not only are all people related but the total cosmos is one interdependent unit in which all the smaller units from human to animal, from vegetable to mineral, and on down to the tiniest particles of electrons and protons, mesons and photons in the cosmic rays, are of one kind. Altogether we are a unified cosmos.

When Unitarians and Universalists merged into one denomination in 1961, they declared themselves to be a living tradition that would draw inspiration from many sources. Besides the major world religions, Humanist teachings, and eventually Pagan or Earth-centered traditions, were included.

Of course, basic theological questions remained: Who am I as a human being? What is my relationship with the universe? What will happen to me when I die?

To express the living tradition, two major changes in theology have taken place: a shift from outer to inner and a shift from supernatural to natural.

The Shift from Outer to Inner

We are trying to come of age as human beings, to give up our dependence on a parental deity enthroned in a supernatural realm. It is not enough to pronounce the patriarchal God dead as some theologians did in the 1960s. We are still faced with those ultimate questions about life and death and meaningful existence. As women came together to study these questions in light of our ancient female religious history, we felt compelled to ask what was the source of our destructive attitudes toward women and the Earth.

Patriarchal societies all over the world have for centuries promulgated a worldview that can be imagined in the form of a ladder. God is at the top, below God are the angels, below them is man, below him is woman, below her are children, and below them is the Earth and its creatures. In this scheme, higher is better, more important, and in control of what is below. The material world, the Earth, and even our own bodies have been seen as inferior to an imaginary supernatural realm where some non-material part of us may go after death if we will just obey the authority above us. The divine in this view resides in the supernatural realm, not the material world.

The biblical tradition gave man dominion over the Earth as well as over women and children. Humanists lopped off God and the angels, but left the rest of the image in place. We have all learned to look upon the Earth as a bundle of resources at the bottom of the ladder, resources to be exploited. Such a worldview undergirds the development of industries that pollute and human relationships that degrade and exploit. It condones and encourages the use of force. It generates resentment, hatred, and war. Those at the top of the ladder are raised to believe that they have to fight to control everyone and everything below them. Those below feel resentment or participate in their own degradation by believing themselves to be inferior.

Scholar and author Naomi Goldenberg suggests that what is needed and is currently happening is the internalization of religion, not only in humans but also in the natural world. As individuals we seek awareness of an immanent divinity or creativity within us as well as to experience an inner spiritual journey toward value and meaning as adults. Contemporary Pagan spirituality helps to provide such an awareness. We speak of the God or Goddess within each of us. Rituals are intended to awaken a heightened sense of wholeness and selfhood. Thou art Goddess, we say to each other. Thou art God. Divinity resides within the person. Since the divine is experienced as internal, it is described in female as well as male terms. Like the Pagans, Unitarian Universalists often describe the divine as internal, as a spiritual journey toward full selfhood, toward an awareness of our creative potential.

This transformation of religion from outer to inner makes each of us responsible for our values. It requires us to become fully aware of our personal and social situation and to articulate that experience. It gives validity to female as well as male experience. It challenges us to alter society whenever it fails to support harmony within the self, among selves, and in relation to nature.

The Shift from Supernatural to Natural

The Earth today is in a severe crisis because of the damage and pollution caused by human beings. Such damage and exploitation flows directly from the biblical belief that nature is fallen and sinful. We have needed to reject that idea. Instead we are beginning to perceive human beings as part of a natural world that has within it the potential for both good and evil. Among Pagans, just as the divine is within human beings as the shape of our creativity, so also is the divine immanent in all of nature. We see ourselves as inter-dependent or connected with every part of the natural world.

Our problem with the Earth has much to do with our fear of death. In the old agrarian traditions, death was a natural part of the life cycle. The dead were thought to become part of the rocks and the trees and the rivers. As male gods took over in mythology and men took over in society, they perceived the goddess of transformation and death to be the most dangerous aspect of the old religions. She was the crone, symbol of the fierce old woman. She had to be destroyed so that death could be conquered. Recycling was no longer good enough. We had to escape the cycle and live forever in some supernatural realm. Earthly life became but a preparation for eternal life. Gradually the Earth, this life, our physical bodies, all became denigrated, compared unfavorably with the life of our so-called immortal souls.

The implications of this denigration of our Earthly life are many. The Earth was no longer sacred. We humans were seen as separate from the rest of life, more important because of our immortal souls. It became easy to see the Earth as a bundle of resources put here for our use. The Earth could be exploited, used, and the loss of our resources not even included in the costs of doing our business. This attitude is carved so deeply into our imaginations that we have been unable even to admit that the holes in the ozone layer, or the pollution of our water and air, will affect us. These were after all only lowly material things. Only our disembodied souls were considered sacred.

Our challenge is to reclaim this Earthly, bodily life as sacred, as the only precious life we have. We are trying to reclaim the image of the old woman who brought transformation and death as a part of the cycle of life. We are trying to stop seeing ourselves as immortal, separate from the rest of life. That means we are trying to stop pitting ourselves against nature because we can't win that way. To destroy the resources of the planet is ultimately to destroy our own life-support system.

To perceive the Earth as sacred means that we celebrate the cycles of nature, the seasons, the waxing and waning of the moon, the life stages of human beings, the potential for creativity and goodness within all. For many Unitarian Universalists, Christmas has become a celebration of the winter solstice and Easter the celebration of spring. In moving away from the idea of a divine savior, we too have returned to the more ancient awareness of religion as our relationship with the cycles of the natural world.

A photograph of the Earth as seen from space might be our mandala. We might meditate on the structure of the atom. We might see the years Jane Goodall spent observing chimpanzees as a spiritual discipline.

To perceive the Earth as sacred means taking seriously our own seventh Principle, approved by our General Assembly in 1985, that we affirm "respect for the interdependent web of all existence *of which we are a part*" (emphasis mine). This Principle was added as part of the process of updating our Principles and Purposes and removing sexist language. It was perhaps the most important thea/ological shift of the late-twentieth century. It means that we do not have dominion over the web, but are a natural part of it. We have also added another line to our Principles and Purposes. It lists one of the sources of our inspiration and wisdom as "spiritual teachings of Earth-centered traditions which celebrate the sacred circle of life and instruct us to live in harmony with the rhythms of nature." We have this precious freedom to draw on many traditions. Pagan or Earth-centered traditions have been crucial in the development of an immanent natural thea/ology. Today we need very much to remind ourselves and proclaim to the world that we look to woman-honoring and Earth-honoring traditions for their special wisdom.

Drumbeats in the Sanctuary

Carole Etzler Eagleheart

It is Sunday morning. Sunlight streams through stained glass windows onto a congregation sitting in pews. But this morning is different. There is no quiet organ music. Instead, from the back of the sanctuary comes the sound of drumbeats, beating to the rhythm of the human heart.

People sit up, suddenly alert, suddenly aware. The drums call to the blood pulsing through their veins. The drums resound through their bodies. The drums call, "Be here. Be here now."

This is one of the gifts of Paganism to Unitarian Universalism: the call to be fully present in the world, to feel the blood pulse, to be aware, to touch the heartbeat of the Earth. It is the gift of embodiment.

In the past there was a gentle joke that Unitarian Universalists were heady people—walking heads without bodies. There was such focus on the mind that it was as if the body did not exist. Sometimes this was even a source of pride, that among all the religious denominations, the UUs were the thinkers. By the 1970s there was growing dissatisfaction with what was seen as cold rationalism. This was the time of the second wave of feminism in the United States. UU women began to question not only the sexist language used in liturgy but also what was seen as a male, left-brain approach to religion.

There was a longing for something beyond words, something that connects the individual directly to the divine, without layers of words delivered from a pulpit. In the 1800s a similar longing for a more intense spiritual experience gave rise to the Transcendentalist movement, a significant branch of our Unitarian heritage. The Transcendentalists became fascinated by Hindu religious texts. They looked beyond Christian and Judaic thought and were open to Pagan influence.

The current wave of Paganism in Unitarian Universalism swept in not with the written word—as it did with Transcendentalism—but with the power of music, particularly the power of drums. I was a traveling musician from 1985 to the end of 2004, visiting UU congregations across the United States. I witnessed a revolution happening: feminist spirituality bursting on the scene, transforming the life of UU congregations.

Women were discovering that we had been robbed. We had been robbed of the image of the divine who looked like us—the Mother Goddess who had been worshipped for thousands of years. We had been robbed of our place as spiritual leaders of her mysteries. Discovery of that theft led first to anger, then to new energy and determination to reclaim what had been lost.

In her important book *When the Drummers Were Women*, Layne Redmond showed us image after image carved in stone, images of women with frame drums leading rituals. The goddesses themselves, such as Cybele, were depicted with the powerful symbol of the drum. "The drum was the means our ancestors used to summon the Goddess," Redmond writes, "and also the instrument through which she spoke."

In those ancient rituals the women drummed and the people danced in a personal experience of the divine. This was not just a wild, primitive pounding. The use of drums and rattles was skillful and intricate. "Creating rhythms powerful enough to move hundreds of people into ecstatic trance states required skilled and disciplined musicians who were well rehearsed," according to Redmond.

Can you imagine the anger that we felt as women when we realized what patriarchal religion had ripped away from us? After just three centuries of Christianity, women went from being religious leaders to being silenced. The Roman Church actually banned the frame drum because of its association with powerful women invoking the Goddess. The drum that had been an instrument of connecting to the sacred feminine became a tool for military organization and conquest. It moved from the energy of the feminine to the warring masculine.

By the end of the fourth century CE, a Christian treatise called "The Teaching of the Three Hundred Eighteen Fathers" declared, "Women are ordered not to speak in church, not even softly, nor may they sing along or take part in responses, but they should only be silent and pray to God."

As Unitarian Universalist women, we read about the history of the suppression of the Goddess and knew it was time to emerge from the silence, not only for our own well-being but for the well-being of the planet. It was time for new language in the songs we sang and the liturgy we used. This was not just about changing God-language so it was no longer masculine. That was only the beginning; it was about opening Unitarian Universalists to an image of the divine that was not just somewhere out in the universe but immanent—earthy and real.

This is an important gift to Unitarian Universalism, especially now, when the Earth is in danger. To feel separate from the Earth, to be focused elsewhere, is to risk ignoring the human actions that are endangering the planet.

As early as the 1970s the music of Carolyn McDade began to touch Unitarian Universalist women with a different vision of our relationship with each other and the Earth. The water ritual she created with Lucille Shuck Longview for the 1980 Women and Religion Continental Convocation began the tradition of water communions that now hold a treasured place in many UU congregations.

As I traveled the United States I could see the women being inspired by Shirley Ranck's *Cakes for the Queen of*

Heaven curriculum. At the time, I remarked on the difference in congregations between what I called BC and
AC—Before *Cakes* and After *Cakes*.

After *Cakes*, UU women were awakened and mobilized.
They gathered not only to read and talk about the Goddess
and her lost history; they began to drum. They began to
dance. At first it was only in private rituals, but then in
wider gatherings. There were conferences like Womanquest
in 1990 in Lake Geneva, Wisconsin, where UU women
came from all over the continent. There was sharing and
visioning and drumming and spiral dancing.

Women came home from experiences like these and
brought the drumming and dancing with them. And they
brought with them a more personal, Earth-centered theology. They began clamoring for opportunities to learn to play
African drums such as the djembe, and even participated in
workshops to make their own drums. They began working
with the rhythms of Middle Eastern frame drums like the
priestesses of long ago. They began to explore the power of
Native American drumming and chanting, and developed
new respect for native peoples who had maintained their
spiritual teachings against great odds. They began asking
questions: Why stick doggedly to nineteenth-century music
when there is such a wealth of ancient and contemporary
music? Why use only one musical instrument like the organ
when the instruments of cultures all over the world are
within reach? Why sit when we can dance? Why mumble
through stiff liturgies when we can tell stories and make art?

These women were not outsiders. They were active members of their UU congregations. They could not be ignored. Suddenly they were demanding different roles for women. They were creating Sunday-morning services that involved the entire body, not just the mind. They were a leading force in opening the door for mixed groups of Pagan women and men to explore and express their beliefs and experiences.

This led some congregations to form chapters of the Covenant of Unitarian Universalist Pagans (CUUPS), where rituals often included drumming and dancing. It is significant that one of the stated purposes of that organization was "encouraging greater use of music, dance, visual arts, poetry, story, and creative ritual in Unitarian Universalist worship and celebration." There is fresh air blowing through that statement. Music, dance, arts—sudden freedom to feel and express and celebrate.

I remember the power of drumming as Margot Adler and Starhawk, invited by CUUPS to attend a UUA General Assembly, led delegates in a spiral dance. For some Unitarian Universalists it was their first experience of Pagan ritual, and the atmosphere was electric. CUUPS convocations introduced UU men and women to Earth-centered music and the influence of Pagan spiritual leaders like Z. Budapest.

Meanwhile, from Vermont to California, from Wisconsin to Texas, Unitarian Universalist women created women's spirituality retreats and conferences where they could explore a new, embodied spirituality. One of my favorites is UU Womenspirit, which was started in 1987 with the goal of encouraging and empowering women to explore their religious and spiritual origins, experiences, and beliefs. The group now holds both spring and fall events at the Mountain Retreat and Learning Center in North Carolina. What these women are able to accomplish is amazing. The workshops are fascinating, and the worship services honoring the Goddess are works of art.

When UU Womenspirit is there, the granite cliffs of the mountain ring with the sound of drumbeats. Women move together in sacred circle dances, like our ancestors danced long ago in ancient rituals. This is one of the places where the gifts of Paganism and Unitarian Universalism meet and embrace. May we continue to create such places of empowerment, embodiment, and joy.

◄o►

CAROLE ETZLER EAGLEHEART *spent twenty years traveling to UU congregations throughout the United States and Canada organizing and performing in concerts, workshops, and Sunday services. She settled in New Mexico, where she became the music director for the Unitarian Universalist Westside Congregation. In 2014, the congregation ordained her as their minister. She is also a writer and composer and has released three songbooks and six recordings of original music.*

DESIGNING RITUAL FOR ALL

MAGGIE BEAUMONT

In the familiar sanctuary, the chairs have been moved.
Instead of the customary rows facing the elevated pulpit,
they are arranged in three concentric circles. In the broad
central space stands an altar bearing stalks of wheat and
tankards of ale. At its four corners, we see a large brass
bell, a cauldron from which fragrant smoke rises, a sparkling goblet of water, and a brilliant geode. In the center,
a flaming chalice.

The congregants file in, looking awkwardly across the
circle at one another, unaccustomed to seeing each other's
faces in worship, but willing to take the risk. From the
eastern corner of the room, someone speaks the familiar
words of opening for Sunday morning, welcoming us to this
congregation and to this celebration of Lammas, the feast
of the first harvest, halfway between the summer solstice's
longest day and the autumn equinox's balance.

In the center, someone else leans toward the altar to light the chalice. A tall flame rises while from the southern corner a new voice says,

> We light this chalice to honor Air, and our holy breath; to honor Fire, and the warmth of our hearts; to honor Water, and the blood that courses in our veins, to honor Earth, and the beauty of our sacred bodies; and to invoke the Spirit of this Beloved Community. We are here together. Blessed be.

Much of the service is familiar: the hymns, the joys and sorrows, the offertory. There is a reading on the cycles of abundance, the nurturing planet, comparing our generosity to breathing as we give to and receive from one another. On this Sunday there is no sermon. Instead, that space is filled by a guided meditation. Before the meditation begins, we pass a basket of fruits and vegetables and ask that each person take one—but don't eat it yet. It's for you to hold while we meditate together. Several voices weave together, taking us on an imaginary journey, exploring our connections to the planet through the food we eat, and our connections to one another through the experiences we share. At the end of the meditation, back in ordinary consciousness, a voice from the western corner of the room invites us to take a bite of what we're holding, if we choose.

After the final hymn, there are plenty of questions over coffee in the lounge.

"Why put the chairs in a circle? What's wrong with the pews we usually sit in?"

"Why such a full altar? Isn't a vase of flowers enough?"

"Why so many different voices? Isn't Sunday worship supposed to be led by the preacher?"

"What does Pagan mean? I thought we were all just Unitarian Universalists."

Unitarian Universalists accustomed to a different style of worship can experience anxiety and disorientation when asked to try a Pagan worship style. At first, they may feel a little alienated, left on the outside because they aren't as familiar with what to do next. Their participation requires a little more effort, a willingness to be the stranger.

But notice that the children are gathered around the altar, asking a different set of questions:

"Can I hold the bell? Are we allowed to ring it?"

"What makes the smoke smell so good?"

"You put the chalice in the center. Can I touch it?"

Pagan ritual is organically multigenerational in ways that traditional Unitarian Universalist worship often struggles to be. Children's worship, or the children's part of an adult service, is often envisioned as watering it down for the little ones. Participatory Pagan worship that engages the senses can be more appealing and inviting to children than a very cerebral traditional worship service. Unitarian Universalists often assume worship is something led by one or a few people who actually do something at the front of the sanctuary, while the group is expected mostly to listen, or even in the case of the best interactive children's story, to answer questions at the whim of the storyteller.

This is not how children best participate. It's not how adults fully participate either, though it's comfortable for many. Effective Pagan ritual, though, aims to engage as much of each participant's whole being as we can.

Children are not yet socialized to spend a lot of their attention on something when they don't see the point. So the first step in designing an inclusive UU Pagan ritual is to be clear about what we intend the ritual to do. Is this a celebration? A gathering to honor the season? Is this a time to do magic to bring a change in consciousness in accordance with will? This is sometimes a hard step to attend to, because we so easily recall previous occasions: "Let's do Persephone's trip to the Underworld. I always like that one." Or, "Let's plant seeds this time. I'm tired of dyeing eggs."

For this multigenerational UU Pagan worship experience we want to create, we must begin with asking what its purpose is. Are we trying to communicate something, teach something, honor something, be present to something, create, celebrate, attract, release, mourn, banish, or what?

What do we want people to feel while the ritual is going on? How do we want them to be feeling when it is over? Is there a shift we want to promote in the way they view the world, or in themselves?

Once we know the purpose, it's time to consider the context.

Is this to be a fully participatory ritual for fifteen or thirty knowledgeable practitioners? A mostly participatory ritual for two hundred or three hundred beginners? Should it be finished in twenty minutes or must it last the full hour? Is the expected congregation mostly children, adolescents, adults, or a mixture? Does everyone speak the same native language? Are there some for whom the language you will offer is a second language, perhaps one that is not well understood yet? Is the expected congregation fairly homogenous as to race, age, class, gender? If yes, why is that? Is it integral to the purpose of this ritual? If no, then who will be present?

Let's think a moment about the ingredients of a successful ritual. I work to engage people on every level to appeal to every sense that I can. We're accustomed, in mainstream America, to talking about the five senses, but it's good to think outside of that box a bit:

Sight includes colors, shapes, patterns, lights. Any of those might be stationary or they might be moving.

Hearing includes words, music, drumming, bells, rhythm, birdsong, wind sounds, whatever the local environment offers.

Smell includes the background smells of a garden in summer, the hungry-making smells of good cooking, the sharp smells of incense, perfume, or compost.

Taste might include a bite of something edible, or it might include something to touch one's tongue.

Touch includes texture, hugs, hand-holding, or a backrub.

Motion or *kinesthetic sense*, often unacknowledged, includes standing up and sitting down, dancing, moving our bodies to the rhythm of music or drum.

Handcrafting includes something to handle, play with, build, or make.

Many rituals include all of these, but even if it's necessary to leave some of them out, the more of them we use, the more powerful the ritual will be and the more likely it is to make genuine change in the participants and the community we share.

With our clear ritual purpose or intention in mind, and an idea of who's going to be present and what senses they share, it is possible to think about the central magical action. Many Unitarian Universalists tell me that magic and magical thinking have no place in a rational world. That's okay, but we'll have a more powerful, transformative ritual if we think about what the central magic is, even if the participants don't necessarily believe in magic. If someone needs to call it a "ritual action" or "creating an intention," that's okay with me, as long as we can agree that it's like acting as if there's no infrared just because we can't see it.

Ideally this will be something each person can do independently, all at the same time, or one after another, depending on how many of us are present. Perhaps we can each write something on a piece of paper and bring it to a central cauldron. Or maybe, as in a Lammas ritual, we will share a symbolic feast, each of us having a sip of ale and a bite of cake.

We must keep asking the question, How will this action serve the intention of the ritual? I'm still surprised at how long this part of the process can take, as we discuss and discard ideas until gradually the right one takes shape. I have the same problem when I'm designing ritual alone, except that it takes longer with only one mind considering the questions.

Once you have the central magical action, the rest of the process of crafting this ritual is designing the pieces that will get us into the central magic, through it, and back out again.

- How do we signal that we're finishing with our arriving and are ready to begin ritual?
- How do we help people leave the cares of the day behind and bring their attention here?
- What will we tell them about the central magic before we do it—instructions, background, a reading, or something else?
- How will we lead them in doing the central magical action—meditation, interactive storytelling with questions and answers, drumming and dancing? Does one person start and the rest follow in turn?
- How will we finish the central magic—back to ordinary consciousness from the meditation? Applause after the story? A blessing on all our work?
- How do we signal that the ritual has ended?

Pagan ritual tends toward a set framework for some of these elements, though the framework varies from one tradition to another as well as from time to time. For one example among many, a typical ritual for one of the groups in which I participate looks like this:

- Cast a circle
- Invite the elements and honor the directions
- Engage in a brief meditation to ground us, connecting to Earth
- Offer a spoken message
- Have each person perform the central magical action at the same time
- Go around the circle, with each person saying whatever we want to say about the work
- Thank the elements and any guests
- Open the circle

It's best to write the talking parts—meditation, homily, sermon, instruction, background, story, whatever—to excite, enlighten, intrigue, or move your adult main-language audience. Then review the individual words for accessibility to the average seven-year-old. Adjust the wording for inclusiveness, but not the concepts, ideas, or stories—allow people to get what they get, while still providing a rich experience for those who can get more. Simpler language is more accessible for all of us anyway, not just for kids or language learners, especially if the first draft includes any technical language or if it references aspects of the culture that some adults might not recognize.

A little explanatory or introductory material will help participants follow the flow. Too much explanation will take them out of the magic of the experiences. I try to acknowledge the different exposures, experiences, and skill levels within the group. It creates understanding, along with the reassurance that it's just fine if anyone follows only part of it.

An Important Note on Accessibility

Making a ritual truly multigenerational isn't only about paying special attention to accessibility for children. We need to be mindful of our elders as well, and this is of special importance for Pagans. Modern Paganism is a relatively young religious category. Several of the largest Pagan traditions in the United States today were founded between 1965 and 1975; many small to medium-sized groups were founded later than that. As a result, most of the founding elders of these traditions are between fifty and eighty years old, including the most prominent Pagan authors and spiritual teachers. They are in the age range in which the ordinary infirmities of age, accident, or illness are most common. At the same time, much of the Pagan ritual work practiced in Unitarian Universalist circles is designed for the able-bodied, even more so than other Unitarian Universalist worship. As a result, it can be all too easy to unintentionally exclude individuals, including our most revered leaders. This has led some UU Pagans to discover that it's far easier to design ritual with accessibility in mind from the start than to figure out, at the last minute, how to make space for someone who cannot do what we had planned. For example, one group I'm in develops its outdoor rituals to include two distinct participation styles in each worship event: one involving walking or dancing and the other involving sitting or lying down. Both groups have activities that are central to the ritual work. Neither group is more important than the other.

Group size is another consideration that necessitates particular attention to physical challenges in Pagan ritual. Longer-established religious groups, including Unitarian Universalists, have long been accustomed to large, imposing physical buildings that house congregations of various sizes. Many of these buildings were constructed in the nineteenth or early-twentieth century, designed by and for bipeds with the typical complement of senses and abilities. Most churches, even today, contain unnecessary barriers and hazards for people who travel on wheels, crutches, walkers, or canes, or who use hearing aids or eyeglasses to improve their ability to interact. But these congregations have tacitly accepted the notion that once a person has lost some important majority-sanctioned ability, they should be willing to stay home and let a family member tell them about it later instead of attending church themselves.

This is always a loss to both the excluded individual and the community, but in Pagan groups the consequences can be debilitating for the group's sustainability. Pagan groups tend to be small. Often only one or two leaders have significant expertise. If we lose one of those, or even if we just make it marginally more difficult for them to attend, we lose not only their participation but also their vital wisdom.

Use microphones if you possibly can. Many hearing aids can pick them up much more easily than unamplified voices. Some rooms have dead spots, but the microphone can make up for that. If possible, have *every* speaker use one, even if it needs to be passed around. Those with hearing challenges—whether with hearing aids or not—will have trouble quickly adjusting to the lower volume and different acoustics of the unamplified voice.

Describe any visuals during the ritual as it is occurring and before it starts. Participants' vision can vary significantly. It is also helpful to offer a written handout or order of service for folks to follow along.

Include alternatives to any action in the ritual for the many levels of ability in a group. Alternatives can be crafted for those who can't stand, sit, march around the room, process outdoors, come forward to the cauldron, breathe the incense, manage pencil and paper, bend down to the floor, chant, or otherwise do the movements you've chosen. Don't skimp on this: Nothing says "You don't count" like being left out of important ritual work.

As much as possible (and yes, please do press for change on this), I always suggest offering public ritual in barrier-free spaces, including the path from ritual space to the bathrooms. Provide chairs of different sizes. Lastly, be sure there are sight lines for people of differing heights.

This isn't an exclusive list, nor has this been an exhaustive discussion. Creating interactive, participatory ritual challenges us to offer ways for people to connect with one another, with the intuitive and unconscious parts of themselves, and with the divine of their understanding.

Inclusive ritual requires that we deliver an experience offering both simplicity and complexity for us all as a way to create greater understanding. There is always a gap between "what I intended" and "what actually happened." Over time I have learned to accept that; I hope you will too.

Blessed be.

◆

MAGGIE BEAUMONT *is a former dean of students of Cherry Hill Seminary and currently serves on the board of trustees of CUUPS. She is a member of Unitarian Universalist congregations in New Jersey and Pennsylvania. She is also a second-degree member of a coven in the Assembly of the Sacred Wheel and a member of the Reclaiming tradition of eclectic Wicca.*

EARTH SONG:
PAGAN CHANT IN UU CHURCHES

NANCY VEDDER-SHULTS

> *Ancient Mother, I hear you calling.*
> *Ancient Mother, I hear your song.*
> *Ancient Mother, I hear your laughter.*
> *Ancient Mother, I taste your tears.*
> —*traditional Neo-Pagan chant*

Singing has always been a powerful vehicle for spirit in my life. Growing up in the Reformed Church of America, I found the choirs at my church to be a source of spiritual nourishment. I deepened my connection to music when I attended the National Women's Music Festival in 1976 and encountered chanting. As a PhD student, fully convinced of the value of rational thinking, I had mystical experiences while singing chants that surprised me and made me reconsider whether rationality was the sole path to personal insight. For the first time since childhood, chanting opened me up to a life in which mystery and wonder existed as real possibilities.

This is exactly what I believe chant can do for Unitarian Universalism: balance mystery and wonder (our first Source) with rationality (our fifth Source). As it did for me, chant can connect Unitarian Universalists to spirit— through their bodies and emotions—to other chanters, and to the Earth. This is the original purpose of religion, since in its initial meaning the word had to do with reconnecting, coming from the Late Latin *religare*, to re-link, to bind back together.

Most cultures on Earth have discovered the spiritual properties of song, many of them devising elaborate systems to tap into these qualities. Taoists in China, Sufis from the Middle East, Jews and Christians in the West, and Buddhists in many parts of the world have all performed simple chants so that their adherents can have mystical experiences through music. All over the world, chant forms a part of religious services—from Hindu mantra and kirtan to Native American drumming and chanting to the "dreamlines" of the aboriginal Australians. As a product of the twentieth and twenty-first centuries, Pagan chant—the chief music of the Neo-Pagan movement—has built on these earlier traditions.

Pagan chant differs from other chanting practices mainly in terms of what it celebrates and advocates: a "greening" of religion that names the Earth as sacred. As a result, the Earth acts as our inspiration as well as the source of our thealogical understanding. Neo-Pagan chants honor the Earth; commemorate the cycle of Her seasons, months, and days; celebrate physical rites of passage; invoke a variety of Earth-based deities; call up the sacred elements of Earth, Air, Fire, and Water; and honor our ancestors. The significance of raising energy within ritual also distinguishes Neo-Pagan chant from that of other religions. Otherwise, Neo-Pagan chant uses the same techniques for creating ecstatic union among its chanters as other traditions.

What every chant tradition knows is that singing these songs relaxes a person into a deep physical place, a meditative state of inner knowing and spiritual openness. Some philosphers and theologians speculate that the reason for this connection of spirit with song is that music is composed of sound vibrations, just like the universe, which is, on the most subatomic level, built not of matter but of energy vibrations. The meditative consciousness that chanting induces expands a person's mind to altered states, through which life's mysteries are more accessible. While chanting, people can access spirit through their bodies and emotions. Chant produces physical and emotional markers that alert singers to the sources of meaning in their lives.

Chant's ability to connect people to their bodies derives from a variety of factors: rhythm, breath, the energy of sound, repetition, and entrainment. Most Pagan chant employs rhythm, often duple meter (e.g., 4/4 time) or waltz time (3/4). The regular beat of such time signatures creates alpha and theta waves in the brain, physiological

changes that often accompany trance and spiritual experiences. The steady pulse of rhythmic chanting functions
like a carrier wave that pulls the scattered pieces of your
mind into a resting place in the core of your being. As you
become centered in your body, you can experience ecstasy
or a feeling of vibrancy and vitality. You stop thinking and
connect with the pulse of the chant.

African drummers realized this long ago, calling the
drumbeats they produced while chanting the "heartbeat
of the earth," a description that Michael Harner affirmed
in his research. Harner, a cultural anthropologist and the
creator of the Foundation of Shamanic Studies, discovered
that the rhythms of shamanic drumming are approximately
the same as the base resonant frequency of the Earth. As a
result, these rhythms connect us to our animal bodies and
to the Earth Herself.

Rhythmic chanting also regulates breathing by opening
up the lungs and synchronizing the breath with the pulse
of the music. Breathing to a chant's beat automatically connects you to your body in a healthy and potentially spiritual
way. While chanting, your breath becomes slower, deeper,
and more even—exactly the qualities that lead to an altered
state of consciousness during meditation.

The reverberation of speech sounds in the body can
also bring a person's awareness back to the physical self.
Vowels in particular generate a variety of resonances in the
body. For this reason, they have been considered sacred in
the traditions of many Western people, including ancient

Egyptians, Greeks, Gnostics, Rosicrucians, and followers of Eastern paths like Nada Yoga. Vowel resonance lays the foundation for Hinduism's use of mantras. According to Thomas Ashley-Farrand in *Healing Mantras*, "Mantra derives its power from the energy effect its sounds produce. Pronouncing a mantra creates a particular physical vibration in the form of the sound that in turn produces various 'energetic effects' in the physical and subtle body."

The repetition of sounds or words in a chant can also create a meditative state while singing. Herbert Benson's pioneering research in *The Relaxation Response* discovered that repeating a simple mantra or nonsense syllable quieted the mind. He found that repeating the syllable "one" succeeded in ridding the mind of extraneous thoughts, feelings, and sensations so that a person could enter the present moment. Such meditative chanting, according to Benson, decreases the heart and respiratory rates, decreases muscle tension, and decreases blood pressure.

The physical and emotional responses to singing chants stem from levels of consciousness that are deeper than conscious rationality. Reason alone cannot explain the peace, trance, and ecstasy that singing chants engenders. I believe that when more rationalist Unitarian Universalists realize the benefits of chant, they will embrace it as we UU Pagans have.

As we've seen, chanting reconnects us with our bodies in healthy, meditative ways that put us in a state of spiritual receptivity. Chant also bonds us with other chanters through the process of entrainment. Entrainment can be defined as synchronizing the body's rhythms with some outside rhythm, for example, when people start tapping their feet absentmindedly while listening to a song. When a group sings together, a type of social entrainment occurs. The singers become a more coherent group, because their bodily rhythms have aligned with one another's. Recent research indicates that there is perhaps no behavior that unites people more strongly than coordinated rhythmic movement.

Unitarian Universalist aloofness toward activities that create unity at the physiological level weakens our movement and keeps us cut off from members of other liberal faiths. For example, if chant were one of our practices, African Americans who come from a gospel tradition that includes a strong focus on movement and song might more readily become our allies and collaborators. I believe that chanting together, and the social entrainment that ensues, will help Unitarian Universalists become more inclusive and create the "ever-widening circles of solidarity and mutual respect" called for in our Principles and Purposes.

Pagan chants draw on the power of influence, or "power-with," as defined by Starhawk, to induce entrainment. And they do so in a preeminently democratic manner, dovetailing with our fifth Unitarian Universalist Principle, "the use of the democratic process within our congregations and in society at large." Chants are arguably the most democratic song form that exists. Almost anyone can sing their simple tunes. They need no conductor, no soloists, no hierarchy of any sort. After singers learn the easy melody and straightforward words of a chant, they can participate comfortably at whatever skill level they have, by singing the tune in unison with others or adding improvised harmonies.

Chant lyrics are also an impetus toward greater unanimity. They affirm what we believe or know to be true. At their core, Pagan chants acknowledge that we are part "of the interdependent web of all existence," the Unitarian Universalist seventh Principle. Each chant is like a mini-story of how humans interwine in the tapestry of life. Singing a chant over and over imprints these stories on our consciousness: "Round and round the Earth is turning / Spring to summer, autumn to winter / And from winter round to spring," "Thank you, Mother Earth," "We all come from the Goddess." After people have sung these chants many times, the songs automatically trigger our unconscious, reminding us in a profound way that we spring from the Earth. Knowing this—not as an intellectual fact but in our physical and emotional selves—UU Pagans have a passionate love of Nature, who is "Mother Earth" or "the Goddess" in Pagan language. Pagan chant can bring the same sense of passion and wonder for our seventh Principle to other Unitarian Universalists as well.

There's a joke in UU circles that we don't sing well because we're too busy reading ahead to see if we agree with the lyrics. But as we've seen, chant involves much more than just rational analysis and judgments about the

words. Using a language of reverence has stirred contro-
versy among Unitarian Universalists in the last decade. As
a result of our denominational history, our hymnal contains
quite a bit of "God language," while "Goddess language"
is comparatively underrepresented. Pagan chant could be
an easy corrective for this imbalance. We need to affirm
the many sources of our living tradition in our music, as
well as equalize male and female names for the sacred. As
I mentally translate *God* to *Goddess* while singing hymns on
Sunday morning, other Unitarian Universalists can participate in Pagan chants while not taking our language literally.

It will help our Humanist and Buddhist brothers and
sisters to realize that *Goddess* is often another term for
Mother Nature, since for them the natural world is as holy
as it is for us UU Pagans. As Rev. David Bumbaugh stated at
a recent General Assembly, "A new language of reverence,
true to our times and rooted in our own experience . . .
reminds us that we are a vulnerable and precious part of a
vulnerable and precious world." To which we UU Pagans
might respond by singing, "The Earth is our Mother. / She
will take care of us. / The Earth is our Mother. / We must
take care of Her."

Pagan chanting can bring our Unitarian Universalist
movement alive. It can solidify our communities, bonding people together in a more cohesive whole. It can unite
people using democratic means. And it can celebrate our
part in the interconnected web of all existence. By singing
Pagan chants we can leave behind the stigma of "God's

frozen people" and begin to integrate body and soul, spirit and rationality, and become the vibrant, liberal religious movement that our country needs.

—◦—

NANCY VEDDER-SHULTS *was named a Wisdom Keeper of the Goddess Spirituality Movement in 2013 for her recording* Chants for the Queen of Heaven *and published* The World Is Your Oracle *in 2017 (Fair Winds Press). She is the thealogical columnist for* SageWoman, *was the musical consultant for* Rise Up & Call Her Name, *and has offered spiritual growth workshops since 1987. See her website at www.mamasminstrel.net.*

Cultural Sharing and Misappropriation

Carol Bodeau

As an Earth-based person and a Unitarian Universalist minister, I have spent many years balancing the joy of sharing inspiration from all our six Sources with the risk of accidentally using others' traditions disrespectfully. One of the greatest blessings of Unitarian Universalism is its inclusiveness: We welcome the diversity of human expression both in our members and in our spiritual modes of expression. Yet this very inclusiveness is one of our greatest challenges. We have been criticized as the "anything goes" religion, and though this is an inaccurate assessment of our theology, it's worth paying attention to the kernel of truth it contains. One of the aspects in which this is most important relates to charges against us of cultural misappropriation, or the misuse of practices, rituals, and tools for which we are not adequately trained or vetted. Indigenous and traditional religious peoples rightly accuse us of using rituals that we do not understand, without the cultural contexts or accountability needed to use them safely or well.

A good example of this occurred in a church where I served many years ago. One Sunday morning, the good-intentioned worship leader invoked the four directions at the *end* rather than at the beginning of the service. Those who understand the theology of invoking the directions know that this is not only an inappropriate use of the ritual, but also energetically and magically risky. You have to invite the directions, the elements, the energies to come in at the beginning of the ritual, and then allow them to leave at the end. Though I wasn't in the sanctuary at the time, someone who understood the situation called me in after the fact to "repair" things. Though the worship leader in this situation intended to honor Earth-based traditions, she simply didn't understand the ritual she was perform-ing. Just because a ritual prayer or tool is included in the hymnal or available on the Internet does not mean we know how to use it correctly. And yet these resources are both valuable and, if used with care, offer us ways to create greater cultural harmony and connection.

So, as we appreciate the benefits of reaching outside our own personal and collective histories for wisdom, we must do so with a deep sense of responsibility. There are important risks in using cultural resources from outside our own traditions. First, we risk violating the needs and wishes of other people whom we wish to treat with honor and respect. We are accountable for respecting other cultures' primary right to their own sacred rituals. We must listen to their requests about when, how, and under what circumstances our use is acceptable. Second, and equally important, we have to be mindful of the dangers of using powerful ritual and spiritual practices in ways that may cause spiritual harm. As we aspire to learn from the many resources and traditions available to us—and so much more is now available thanks to the Internet—we must attend to the complex and delicate work of doing so safely and appropriately. My own journey into Unitarian Universalist religious leadership is an example of the messiness of this journey. I have made more mistakes than I can count, but I believe that the lessons I have learned have been more than worth the struggle. Whether we are celebrating an interfaith Passover Seder, creating a circle ritual for Beltane or Samhain, or honoring the Christian Easter season while remaining respectful of our atheist congregants, we are called to truly balance our *interest in* and our *respect for* other cultures.

I came to Unitarian Universalism after years as a college professor, with a PhD in American literature and Native American studies. I had taught Native American studies in both community, college, and university settings, and had some experience with the tricky terrain of being a woman of Scots-Irish-French lineage working with native issues. Through this experience, I've learned that it is important to only speak on these issues with my own voice—to never attempt to speak for a native person—and to avoid the dangerous pitfalls of romanticizing other peoples. Too often, those with the privilege of the dominant culture minimize the existing power of others through a sense of pity, a feeling that *they* need our "help." Another key indicator of privilege in action is idealizing the non-dominant group. By the time I came to Starr King School for the Ministry, I understood these principles in political and academic contexts but had not yet translated them to the religious arena. This, I was to discover, was where much of the work for our tradition, and for me personally, was to be done.

As is true for many Unitarian Universalists, the spiritual experiences of my life would not fit into the boxes provided to me by my culture. I was born intuitive, able to communicate with the natural world directly, and able to use energy to heal myself and others, all things not included in typical Western religions. Like many Westerners with these gifts, my magical experiences in nature led me to explore Earth-centered traditions. I was particularly drawn to the teachings of the native peoples of the Great Lakes, where I grew up. I studied Potawatomi, Ojibwa, and Iroquois history, culture, and cosmologies, first on my own, then as an anthropology minor in college. As a graduate student, I focused my work on colonial European interactions with East Coast tribes and began teaching from this perspective. Meanwhile, during my graduate studies, I also began working with cross-cultural Earth-based teachers and indigenous spiritual teachers. When I began seminary, I was completely unaware of the gaps in my understanding of how these two paths—the intellectual/academic and the spiritual—needed to intersect and work together. Not unlike other Unitarian Universalists, I had a sense that my intellectual endeavors and successes trumped any unconscious weaknesses I might have in the realm of religious accountability.

Overcoming this bias of favoring the academic over the religious is essential to our spiritual and social maturity. During my first weeks at Starr King, I experienced my first lesson in the complexity of cultural sharing in a spiritual setting. During a class that I was asked to help lead, I shared a prayer that I had been taught by a Native American teacher. One of the leaders of the class was deeply troubled by this and refused to participate. I was shocked. This prayer had been shared by a native teacher who expected me to share it with others, and I had never considered it to be wrong or inappropriate to speak it. That same week, I attended a Starr King workshop on cultural misappropriation, and during it my own native teacher was named as an example of native teachers' selling their culture in a "bad" way to regain power from the white culture. To say that I was thrown into a tailspin would be an understatement. But in the way of a magical universe, I was to spend that same weekend with my teacher (whom I only saw in person a few weeks out of the year). And I asked her what she thought about it all.

I learned in that conversation that cultural sharing is complex for people on all sides of the exchange. Not only was I considered suspect by some for receiving teachings that were not from my own genetic/historical culture, but my teacher was herself considered suspect by some in her community for sharing wisdom. And yet, many others in the native community supported and respected her sharing, as well. This is a central lesson: Attitudes toward cultural sharing are subjective, and pro and con statements cannot be assigned in any general way to racial or cultural groups. We cannot in any general way say that all native or indigenous peoples are offended by non-natives using spiritual practices that mirror their traditional ways. Nor can we say that all white people think widespread, careless use of others' traditions is acceptable. So how do we make sense of this subjective experience of cultural sharing?

That question has been at the center of my spiritual and religious journey. After many conversations with seminarians, both native and non-native, and with lay leaders, I began to describe Paganism and Earth-based practice as the new "closet" of Unitarian Universalism, because so many people were afraid to come out as Earth-based. I talked with many people who felt their spirituality closely mirrored that of ancient and contemporary Earth-based peoples. Yet they felt terrified of doing it wrong and getting in trouble for stealing other people's traditions. Their Unitarian Universalism was catching them in a double bind: How could they truly engage the six Sources, and the wisdom of others' religious history and knowledge, while still practicing just and respectful relations with other cultural communities? It's a conundrum to which there is no one, simple, easy answer. Yet despite the difficulties of the path, it is a valuable journey that we can indeed take gracefully.

Religious learning happens in stages; we do not step into a new tradition fully mature and able to handle the complexities of that tradition. We begin with simplistic half-understandings and incomplete perceptions. We must learn in steps, just as children do when learning their own religious cultures from family and community. In a conversation with then-president of Starr King Rebecca Parker, I explained this by saying that the trinket-ization phase of religious learning—in which we oversimplify the meaning and importance of objects and ritual words as separate from their context—which characterizes so much immature cultural misappropriation is like an early stage of religious learning that all small children go through. When a child is learning her own religion or culture, she begins with simple symbols and spoken mantras or prayers. In Unitarian Universalism, a preschooler knows the chalice is important but is unlikely to understand the complex history and theology behind the symbol. He may know how to name a few of the seven Principles but not how to really understand them deeply. The same is true of adults stepping into new traditions. I explained to Rebecca Parker that as non-native people attempt to learn and integrate the deep Earth-centered wisdom of indigenous cultures, from both the past and the present, we will be like children. We will make mistakes, misunderstand things, and need guidance to develop theological and spiritual maturity in these areas. This in no way excuses cultural misappropriation or disrespect, though.

So how to strike the balance of actively learning valuable ways of thinking and being, while still honoring others' cultures and traditions? One solution that is often offered is for European peoples to focus only on the spiritual traditions of their genetic ancestors. In other words, white people should study the traditions of northern Europe.

At the 2005 General Assembly in Fort Worth, Native American theologian George Tinker offered this solution. And while I respect his perspective, his words triggered a deep awareness in me. How could I, as an Earth-centered person, connect with land I had never touched? At the time of his talk, I had never been on Irish or Scottish soil. If my religion is based on a connection to the Earth itself, to the land and trees and plants of my place, I could only do that *on land I actually knew*. The wisdom teachers who knew my landscape were native to the Great Lakes. For me, the elementary-school stage of my spiritual journey required just simply connecting to the land I was actually living on—first, Michigan, and then later California—and learning from people who connected spiritually to that specific land.

A few years later, at a Liberal Religious Educators Association conference in Sacramento, California, I heard Sobonfu Some, a spiritual teacher of the Dagara tribe from Senegal, speak about returning to our ancestors. By then, I had matured some along my spiritual path; I was ready for this more complex connection to the land of my ancestors. My connection to the Earth itself was strong enough; I had learned enough about how to be a part of the circle of life physically, intellectually, and theologically that I could begin to explore my own ancestral connections to other lands in other places. But I am aware that, even then, it was a matter of economic privilege that allowed me to travel to Scotland and begin that process. Many, many people whose ancestors come from parts of the world beyond the land they inhabit have no access to the land of their genetic ancestors.

There is no simple way to replace an ancient connection to the land of your ancestors once it has been lost. So those of us searching for spiritually rich connections outside the physical places where we were born are bound to find the journey messy and complicated. Yet we mustn't give up the effort to connect to the land, and to the ancient wisdom of magic and energy that are alive there, offering powerful change and transformation. Connection to the land—a deep, spiritual sense of the magic of place, of nature imbued with active divinity—is incredibly powerful and sacred. I believe it is all that will save us, and our planet home. So the journey from spiritual child to adult is both necessary and incredibly powerful.

As we leave behind the oversimplifications of purely symbolic and romanticized religious rituals, as we learn to explore and honor the deeper theologies and cultural models upon which those rituals and symbols are based, we must become mature allies of the people who share them. This, it seems to me, is the most essential step in our spiritual maturation. If we are to explore and engage the diversity of the world's religious traditions, we must do so as conscious, active allies of those peoples from whom we wish to learn. Too often, we see their teachings as commodities we can purchase at a bookstore or a workshop. We eagerly embrace the simplified version of their hard-earned wisdom, gathered often through centuries of struggle and near-extinction, without any connection to their communities or their *contemporary* lived experiences. We must recognize our teachers of all traditions as members of our human family, whose destiny is tied to our own. We must wake up to the contemporary experiences of present-day tribal peoples, if their teachings are important to us. We must begin to act as if we are engaged in *sharing*, in a *true exchange* of energies. Just as we hope to learn from others' ancient wisdoms—be they Native American, Celtic, African, Asian, or any other—we must build real and living relationships with those communities. And we must do this from a place of equality and respect, as allies who respond to requests based on each culture's self-stated needs and desires, rather than from our own ideas of "helping." Finally, if we have received spiritual tools, teachings, or rituals, we must us ask ourselves if they were given as gifts, given with love and permission, or if we have bought them or taken them outside the context of relationship. For it is only in the context of real relationship that we can share them appropriately.

I have come to understand that *all* Earth's people and creatures suffer from the legacy of colonialism. Just as the native peoples of the world suffered immeasurable loss of life, culture, and place through the invasion of European dominating powers, so too do the descendants of those colonials experience dislocation and alienation from their deep spiritual and cultural roots. We are searching, many of us, for connection to a richer heritage than what we were given by our communities, and for a deep connection to the Earth herself. In this, we are true allies with all peoples, for we all share one home planet.

A core Pagan concept is the oneness of all life, no matter the species or location. Whatever our ethnic heritage may be, we are all one family and we have only one home to share. So no matter how complex the task of honoring diversity may be, embracing this unity is of the utmost importance to us all. It is life-affirming and life-saving, both for us as individuals and for the whole of our species and the Earth herself. The spiritual wisdom and richness offered by loving teachers of Earth-based traditions may save us all. Let us take the journey of honoring them with an attitude of mutuality, respect, and deep gratitude. Let us act as responsible allies, members of one family of life, together sharing hope for a brighter future. May it be so.

—<o>—

CAROL BODEAU is minister of the Westside Unitarian Universalist Church in Knoxville, Tennessee. She has been practicing Earth-based and mystical spiritual traditions for more than thirty years. In addition to her church ministry, she works as an energy healer, coach, and ritual leader. She honors the traditions of her many teachers, including elders from the Native North American, African, Kabbalist, and cross-cultural shamanic traditions.

Glossary

Altar. A table, stone, or surface on which to place the tools for worship and reflection. The objects on the altar vary depending on the tradition, sect, or denomination of Paganism or Earth-centered religions.

Book of Shadows. A book of sacred blessings, poetry, chants, benedictions, opening words, prayers, rituals, and personal reflections created by a solitary or a group.

Circle. A gathering of people for worship in which they sit or stand in a circle. A sacred space.

Coven. A group of people who meet on a regular basis to practice their beliefs with ritual and ceremony.

Druid. A priest, magician, or soothsayer in the ancient Celtic religion.

Elements. The sacred components of nature: Air (communication and intuition), Fire (passion and change), Water (dreams), Earth (roots and grounding), and Spirit.

Esbats. Sacred times to gather in accordance with the phases of the moon.

Full Moon. When the moon is full, it is a perfect occasion for sacred works and for drawing on favorable energy in ceremonies and rituals.

God/Goddess. Representations of the divine energies of all creation recognizing the essence of divine masculine and feminine energies.

Initiate. A person who takes on the responsibility of being in service to a particular tradition, sect, or denomination.

Lady/Lord. Terms for the divine feminine and masculine. In older traditions these are titles bestowed on longtime priests and priestesses.

Magic or Magick. The science of managing energies and intentions through ritual, ceremony, or prayer consciously directed to accomplish a result.

Neo-Paganism. A contemporary religious movement that seeks to incorporate traditions outside of the main world religions, and to follow a set of nature-based beliefs and practices, both ancient and modern.

New Moon. A moon phase used for personal growth, healing, and blessing new ventures or projects. A time to consecrate tools and objects to use during rituals, ceremonies, or an upcoming event.

Occult. From the Latin *occulere*, "to conceal" that which is hidden behind outer appearances. In Western philosophies, it is the use of nature to develop psychic skills and investigate ancient mysteries and philosophies for the purpose of spiritual growth and enlightenment.

Pagan. From the Latin *Paganus*. In classical Latin, "villager, rustic, civilian," from *pagus* "rural district." Historically, Christianity flourished in cities, while in rural areas country people held onto their more ancient traditions. These traditions eventually were labeled *pagan* because they were practiced mostly in rural areas. Over many centuries, *pagan* became a derogatory term meaning "non-Christian." Today it simply means one who adheres to the ancient rural traditions.

Sabbat. Eight festivals or holy days of the agricultural calendar for Pagans. Celebrating the movement of life through the calendar.

Spell. A focused prayer, recited during a ritual or a spiritual ceremony.

Thea/ology. A neologism derived from ancient Greek, the term is generally understood as a discourse that reflects upon the meaning of Goddess (*thea*) in addition to God (*theo*). *Thealogy* is the study and reflection upon the feminine divine from a feminist perspective while *theology* is the study of the nature of the masculine divine. The combined form of the two words indicates a feminist orientation to the traditional study of the divine and religion.

Tradition. Teachings received from a family, clan, group, organization, cultural group, or ancestor, most often handed down orally, or rewritten by hand from a central book into one's own book of shadows.

Triple Goddess. Aspects of the Goddess—the maiden, mother, and crone—represented by the three phases of the moon: waxing, full, and waning.

Wicca. In modern contexts, the word traces to English folklorist Gerald Gardner (1884–1964). His followers created the tradition of Wicca as a form of Witchcraft. Today it encompasses a variety of traditions from orthodox practices to liberal eclectic versions.

Witch. Any person, female or male, who practices the science of using energy to bend and craft one's intentions to manifest in the world. The term refers to a person who practices magick with religion, as opposed to one who only practices magick.

Witchcraft. An Indo-European mystical religion that was first declared to be a crime in England in 1542. Witch trials peaked in the 1580s and 1640s, falling sharply after 1660. The Witchcraft Act was not fully repealed in Great Britain until 1951. This book discusses Witchcraft as a religion or spiritual path with a common set of nature-based beliefs and practices that are in harmony and balance with natural-world surroundings, and that reflect an understanding that all things are connected on the physical and spiritual level. Today's Witchcraft traditions sprouted from Great Britain, however there are many new ones in the U.S., embracing many cultural roots.

Resources

Books

Classics

Adler, Margot. *Drawing Down the Moon: Witches, Druids, Goddess-Worshippers, and Other Pagans in America.* New York: Penguin Books, 2006.

Berger, Helen A. *A Community of Witches: Contemporary Neo-Paganism and Witchcraft in the United States.* Columbia, SC: University of South Carolina Press, 1999.

Clifton, Chas S. *Witchcraft Today, Book I: The Modern Craft Movement.* St. Paul, MN: Llewellyn Publications, 1997.

Clifton, Chas S. *Witchcraft Today, Book II: Modern Rites of Passage.* St. Paul, MN: Llewellyn Publications, 1995.

Clifton, Chas S. *Witchcraft Today, Book III: Witchcraft and Shamanism.* St. Paul, MN: Llewellyn Publications, 1994.

Crowley, Vivianne. *Principles of Paganism*. London: Thorsons, 1996.

Cuhulain, Kerr. *The Law Enforcement Guide to Wicca*. Victoria, BC: Horned Owl Publishing, 1997.

Cunningham, Scott. *Wicca: A Guide for the Solitary Practitioner*. St. Paul, MN: Llewellyn Publications, 1989.

Hutton, Ronald. *The Triumph of the Moon: A History of Modern Pagan Witchcraft*. Oxford: Oxford University Press, 2001.

Montley, Patricia. *In Nature's Honor: Myths and Rituals Celebrating the Earth*. Boston: Skinner House, 2005.

Starhawk. *Dreaming the Dark: Magic, Sex, and Politics*. Boston: Beacon Press, 1997.

Starhawk. *The Spiral Dance: A Rebirth of the Ancient Religion of the Great Goddess*. New York: HarperOne, 1999.

Starhawk. *Truth or Dare: Encounters with Power, Authority, and Mystery*. New York: HarperCollins, 1988.

Starhawk, M. Macha Nightmare and the Reclaiming Collective. *The Pagan Book of Living and Dying: Practical Rituals, Prayers, Blessings, and Meditations on Crossing Over*. New York: HarperOne, 1997.

Families

Campanelli, Pauline. *Ancient Ways: Reclaiming Pagan Traditions*. St. Paul, MN: Llewellyn Publications, 1991.

Campanelli, Pauline. *Wheel of the Year: Living the Magical Life*. St. Paul, MN: Llewellyn Publications, 1989.

Johnson, Cait and Maura D. Shaw. *Celebrating the Great Mother: A Handbook of Earth-Honoring Activities for Parents and Children*. Rochester, VT: Destiny Books, 1995.

Monaghan, Patricia. *Magical Gardens: Myth, Mulch and Marigolds*. St. Paul, MN: Llewellyn Publications, 1997.

O'Gaea, Ashleen. *The Family Wicca Book: The Craft for Parents & Children*. St. Paul, MN: Llewellyn Publications, 1994.

Stafford, Anika. Aisha's Moonlit Walk: Stories and Celebrations for the Pagan Year. Boston: Skinner House, 2005.

Starhawk, Diane Baker and Anne Hill. *Circle Round: Raising Children in Goddess Traditions*. New York: Bantam Books, 2000.

Starhawk, M. Macha Nightmare and the Reclaiming Collective. *The Pagan Book of Living and Dying: Practical Rituals, Prayers, Blessings, and Meditations on Crossing Over*. New York: HarperOne, 1997.

Africa and African Diaspora

Neimark, Philip John. *The Way of the Orisa: Empowering Your Life through the Ancient African Religion of Ifa*. New York: HarperOne, 1993.

Olupona, Jacob K. *African Traditional Religions in Contemporary Society*. St. Paul, MN: Paragon House, 1998.

Pinckney, Roger. *Blue Roots: African-American Folk Magic of the Gullah People, Second Edition*. Orangeburg, SC: Sandlapper Publishing, 2003.

Somé, Malidoma Patrice. *Ritual: Power, Healing and Community*. New York: Penguin Books, 1997.

Teish, Luisah. *Jambalaya: The Natural Woman's Book of Personal Charms and Practical Rituals*. New York: HarperOne, 1988.

Teish, Luisah. *Jump Up: Good Times Throughout the Season with Celebrations from Around the World*. Berkeley, CA: Conari Press, 2000.

Thompson, Robert Farris. *Flash of the Spirit: African and Afro-American Art and Philosophy*. New York: Vintage Books, 1984.

The Americas

Deloria Jr., Vine. *God Is Red: A Native View of Religion, 30th Anniversary Edition*. Golden, CO: Fulcrum Publishing, 2003.

Dog, Leonard Crow and Richard Erdoes. *Crow Dog: Four Generations of Sioux Medicine Men*. New York: Harper Perennial, 1996.

Asia and the Pacific

Duerr, Hans Peter. *Dreamtime: Concerning the Boundary between Wilderness and Civilization*. New York: Blackwell Publishers, 1985.

Sarangerel. *Riding Windhorses: A Journey into the Heart of Mongolian Shamanism*. Rochester, VT: Destiny Books, 2000.

Pan-European

Aswynn, Freya. *Northern Mysteries & Magick: Runes and Feminine Powers, Second Edition*. St. Paul, MN: Llewellyn Publications, 2002.

Leland, Charles G. and Mario Pazzaglini. *Aradia: Or the Gospel of the Witches, Expanded Edition*. Blaine, WA: Phoenix Publishing, 1999.

Celtic Spirit

De Grandis, Francesca. *Be a Goddess! A Guide to Celtic Spells and Wisdom for Self-Healing, Prosperity and Great Sex*. New York: HarperOne, 1998.

Hopman, Ellen Evert and Lawrence Bond. *People of the Earth: The New Pagans Speak Out*. Rochester, VT: Inner Traditions, 1995.

Hutton, Ronald. *The Triumph of the Moon: A History of Modern Pagan Witchcraft*. Oxford: Oxford University Press, 2001.

Matthews, Caitlin and John Matthews. *The Encyclopedia of Celtic Wisdom: A Celtic Shaman's Sourcebook*. Shaftesbury, UK: Element Books Ltd., 1994.

Orr, Emma Restall. *Spirits of the Sacred Grove: The World of a Druid Priestess*. New Alresford, UK: Moon Books, 2014.

Stewart, R.J. *Earth Light: The Ancient Path to Transformation, Rediscovering the Wisdom of Celtic and Faery Lore*. Lake Toxaway, NC: Mercury Publishing, 1998.

Celtic History, Myth, and Folklore

Anderson, William. *Green Man: The Archetype of Our Oneness with the Earth*. San Francisco: Harper San Francisco, 1990.

Carmichael, Alexander. *Carmina Gadelica: Hymns & Incantations*. Edinburgh: Floris Books, 1994.

Hutton, Ronald. *The Pagan Religions of the Ancient British Isles: Their Nature and Legacy*. Oxford: Blackwell Publishers, 1993.

Jones, Prudence and Nigel Pennick. *A History of Pagan Europe*. Abingdon, UK: Routledge, 1997.

Piggott, Stuart. *The Druids*. London: Thames & Hudson, 1985.

Stewart, R.J. *Celtic Gods Celtic Goddesses*. London: Cassell Illustrated, 1992.

Stewart, R.J. *Celtic Myths, Celtic Legends*. London: Blandford Publishing, 1994.

Men's Mysteries

Anderson, William. *Green Man: The Archetype of Our Oneness with the Earth.* San Francisco: Harper San Francisco, 1990.

Bly, Robert. *Iron John: A Book About Men, Third Edition*. Boston: Da Capo Press, 2015.

Campbell, Joseph. *The Hero with a Thousand Faces*. Novato, CA: New World Library, 2008.

Cuhulain, Kerr. *Wiccan Warrior: Walking a Spiritual Path in a Sometimes Hostile World*. St. Paul, MN: Llewellyn Publications, 2000.

Evans, Arthur. *Witchcraft and the Gay Counterculture.* Boston: Fag Rag Books, 1978.

Farrar, Janet, and Stewart Farrar. *The Witches' God: Lord of the Dance*. London: Robert Hale Ltd., 1989.

Hay, Harry. *Radically Gay: Gay Liberation in the Words of Its Founder*. Boston: Beacon Press, 1996.

Women's Mysteries

Budapest, Zsuzsanna. *Summoning the Fates: A Woman's Guide to Destiny*. New York: Three Rivers Press, 1999.

Curott, Phyllis. *Book of Shadows: A Modern Woman's Journey into the Wisdom of Witchcraft and the Magic of the Goddess*. New York: Three Rivers Press, 1999.

Ehrenreich, Barbara and Deirdre English. *Witches, Midwives and Nurses: A History of Women Healers*. New York: The Feminist Press, 2010.

Eisler, Riane. *The Chalice and the Blade: Our History, Our Future*. New York: HarperOne, 1988.

Eisler, Riane and David Loye. *The Partnership Way: New Tools for Living & Learning, Healing Our Families, and Our World*. San Francisco: Harper San Francisco, 1990.

Eisler, Riane. *Sacred Pleasure: Sex, Myth, and the Politics of the Body—New Paths to Power and Love*. New York: HarperOne, 1996.

Farrar, Janet, and Stewart Farrar. *The Witches' Goddess: The Feminine Principle of Divinity*. London: Robert Hale Ltd., 1999.

Gimbutas, Marija. *The Goddesses and Gods of Old Europe*. Berkeley: University of California Press, 2007.

Gimbutas, Marija. *The Language of the Goddess: UnEarthing the Hidden Symbols of Western Civilization*. New York: Harper & Row, 1989.

Johnson, Buffie. *Lady of the Beasts: The Goddess and Her Sacred Animals*. Rochester, VT: Inner Traditions, 1994.

Lubell, Winifred Milius. *The Metamorphosis of Baubo: Myths of Woman's Sexual Energy*. Nashville, TN: Vanderbilt University Press, 1994.

Neumann, Erich. *The Great Mother: An Analysis of the Archetype*. Princeton, NJ: Princeton University Press, 2015.

Paris, Ginette. *Pagan Grace: Dionysus, Hermes, and Goddess Memory in Daily Life*. Washington, D.C.: Spring Publications, 1998.

Paris, Ginette. *Pagan Meditations: The Worlds of Aphrodite, Artemis and Hestia*. Washington, D.C.: Spring Publications, 1998.

Pollack, Rachel. *The Body of the Goddess: Sacred Wisdom in Myth, Landscape and Culture*. Shaftesbury, UK: Element Books Ltd., 1997.

Qualls-Corbett, Nancy. *The Sacred Prostitute: Eternal Aspect of Feminine*. Toronto: Inner City Books, 1988.

Ranck, Shirley Ann. *Cakes for the Queen of Heaven: An Exploration of Women's Power Past, Present, and Future*. New York: Authors Choice Press, 2006.

Reilly, Patricia Lynn. *A God Who Looks Like Me: Discovering a Woman-Affirming Spirituality*. New York: Ballantine Books, 1995.

Sjoo, Monica and Barbara Mor. *The Great Cosmic Mother: Rediscovering the Religion of the Earth*. New York: HarperOne, 1987.

Stange, Mary Zeiss. *Woman the Hunter*. Boston: Beacon Press, 1998.

Starhawk. *The Spiral Dance: A Rebirth of the Ancient Religion of the Great Goddess*. New York: HarperOne, 1999.

Stone, Merlin. *Ancient Mirrors of Womanhood: A Treasury of Goddess and Heroine Lore from Around the World*. Boston: Beacon Press, 1990.

Stone, Merlin. *When God Was a Woman*. New York: Houghton Mifflin Harcourt, 1978.

Walker, Barbara G. *The Crone: Woman of Age, Wisdom, and Power*. New York: Harper Collins, 1988.

Walker, Barbara G. *The Skeptical Feminist: Discovering the Virgin, Mother, and Crone*. New York: Harper Collins, 1988.

Walker, Barbara G. *The Woman's Dictionary of Symbols and Sacred Objects*. New York: HarperOne, 1988.

Walker, Barbara G. *The Woman's Encyclopedia of Myths and Secrets*. New York: HarperOne, 1983.

Wolkstein, Diane and Samuel Noah Kramer. *Inanna: Queen of Heaven and Earth—Her Stories and Hymns from Sumer*. New York: Harper & Row, 1983.

Magazines

SageWoman
SageWoman.com

Witches and Pagans
WitchesandPagans.com

Websites

Covenant of Unitarian Universalist Pagans
CUUPS.org

Nature's Path—Celebrating UU-Paganism and Earth-Centered Experience
patheos.com/blogs/naturespath

Circle Sanctuary
CircleSanctuary.org

The Witches' Voice
Witchvox.com

Covenant of the Goddess
COG.org

Reclaiming Collective
reclaiming.org

Starhawk
starhawk.org

Ár nDraíocht Féin: A Druid Fellowship
ADF.org

The Wild Hunt
WildHunt.org

Pagan Pride Project
PaganPride.org

Pagan Federation
PaganFed.org

Z. Budapest
zbudapest.com

Cakes for the Queen of Heaven
cakesforthequeenofheaven.org

Rise Up & Call Her Name
riseupandcallhername.com

Unitarian Universalist Women's Federation
uuwf.org

Joseph Campbell Foundation
jcf.org